Praise for *Star for Jesus (And Other Jobs I Quit)*

"For anyone seeking solace from the exhausting cycle of proving their worth, *Star for Jesus* is an invaluable and hilarious companion, pointing you to the transformative power of embracing God's unconditional love and grace."

—Jennifer Dukes Lee, author of
Growing Slow and *Stuff I'd Only Tell God*

"Warm, witty, and infinitely relatable, the stories on these pages invite us to stop striving and start accepting the unforced rhythms of grace that God so graciously offers us. Kimberly Stuart is a natural-born storyteller who has given us a gem of a book to guide us toward glimmers of grace in our messy, real lives."

—Kayla Craig, creator of Liturgies for Parents and
author of *Every Season Sacred* and *To Light Their Way*

"Kim Stuart is one of the most delightful humans we know—buoyant but deep, hilarious but tender—and that same spirit flows through these pages. This book is a personal but universal guide to releasing the tidy and simplistic life of faith we thought we should live in order to receive a messier, grace-filled, transcendent life of faith that actually is."

—Katherine and Jay Wolf, coauthors of
Hope Heals and *Suffer Strong*

"*Star for Jesus (And Other Jobs I Quit)* is a great book, beautifully written by an author who isn't afraid to dig a little deeper to discover a life that matters. Through the telling of thoughtful, nostalgic, and very funny stories, we are reminded that the secret to living a life full of meaning is found in the Giver of endless grace."

—Maria Goff, wife, mother, grandmother,
and author of *Love Lives Here*

STAR FOR
JESUS
(AND OTHER
JOBS I QUIT)

STAR FOR JESUS
(AND OTHER JOBS I QUIT)

REDISCOVERING THE GRACE
THAT SETS US FREE

KIMBERLY STUART

WORTHY
— PUBLISHING —

New York • Nashville

Worthy Books

Hachette Book Group

1290 Avenue of the Americas, New York, NY 10104

worthypublishing.com

twitter.com/WorthyPub

First Edition: March 2024

Worthy Books is a division of Hachette Book Group, Inc. The Worthy Books name and logo are trademarks of Hachette Book Group, Inc.

The publisher is not responsible for websites (or their content) that are not owned by the publisher.

The Hachette Speakers Bureau provides a wide range of authors for speaking events. To find out more, go to hachettespeakersbureau.com or email HachetteSpeakers@hbgusa.com.

Worthy books may be purchased in bulk for business, educational, or promotional use. For information, please contact your local bookseller or the Hachette Book Group Special Markets Department at special.markets@hbgusa.com.

Scripture quotations marked NLT are taken from the *Holy Bible*, New Living Translation, copyright ©1996, 2004, 2015 by Tyndale House Foundation. Used by permission of Tyndale House Publishers, Inc., Carol Stream, Illinois 60188. All rights reserved.

Scripture quotations marked AMPC are taken from the Amplified® Bible, Copyright © 1954, 1958, 1962, 1964, 1965, 1987 by The Lockman Foundation. Used by permission. lockman.org.

Print book interior design by Bart Dawson

Library of Congress Cataloging-in-Publication Data

Names: Stuart, Kimberly, 1975- author.

Title: Star for Jesus (and other jobs I quit) : rediscovering the grace that sets us free / Kimberly Stuart.

Description: First edition. | New York : Worthy, 2024.

Identifiers: LCCN 2023041004 | ISBN 9781546004721 (hardcover) | ISBN 9781546004745 (ebook)

Subjects: LCSH: Grace (Theology). | Perfectionism (Personality trait)--Religious aspects--Christianity. | Forgiveness--Religious aspects--Christianity. | Interpersonal relations--Religious aspects--Christianity.

Classification: LCC BT761.3 .S78 2024 | DDC 234--dc23/eng/20231114

LC record available at https://lccn.loc.gov/2023041004

ISBNs: 9781546004721 (hardcover), 9781546004745 (ebook)

Printed in the United States of America

LSC-C

Printing 1, 2024

To Marc, Ana, Mitchell, and Thea,
for showing me grace upon grace.

And to my parents, Randy and Patti,
my first and best teachers of the stubborn love of Jesus.

CONTENTS

CONTENTS

FOREWORD

by Bob Goff

I TURNED SIXTEEN AND IMMEDIATELY GOT MY DRIVER'S license. I still had birthday cake on my chin when my parents took the keys out of the jar where they had done a bad job hiding them for six months and slid them across to my side of the table. I was young, so I didn't have much in the way of maturity, but I now had wheels and knew there would be many adventures ahead of me.

My first car was a blue Volkswagen Beetle. It had a few miles on it and a dent on the back fender, but it fit me, and there was room for my backpack on the rear seat. I had planned for at least a year to go hiking in the Sierra Mountains when I started driving, and a few days later had a long weekend and gas money, so I hit the road. It didn't give me any pause that I had no experience on the highway and hadn't gone anywhere alone yet. At sixteen years and four days old, I took my newfound freedom out for a spin and headed to the mountains.

I got on the highway headed east toward Lake Tahoe. The sunroof was open, and the wind blew through my fire-engine-red hair as I merged into traffic. It was just me, my backpack, and Crosby, Stills, Nash and Young playing on the eight-track tape player in the dash (I am actually that old). It wasn't long before I was a little bored and noticed there was an eighteen-wheel truck just ahead of me in the middle lane pulling a huge cargo trailer. I wondered whether if I got within a few feet of the back bumper if the vortex of wind created behind the truck was strong enough to suck me, my backpack, my Volkswagen, and my flaming red hair along. And you know what? It worked. I know, I know—no brains, no headache.

Looking back, I learned several important lessons that day. First, I figured out why sixteen-year-olds are virtually impossible to insure. I also learned something about the power of big moving objects to create a space behind them that pulls everything nearby along. And finally, I learned that experiencing all this power would require me to move a little closer.

Grace can be like an immense moving object in our lives, and if we are willing to get close enough to it, everyone and everything we encounter will be drawn along in the vortex it creates. This is a book about the power of grace in the world. It is an invitation to take your most extravagant version of grace out on the road for a spin and see what it can do in your life and the lives of the ones nearby.

Kim has been a friend of mine for a long time. She is equal parts fun, sassy, and stunningly humble. She has the ability with her words to call us out on our missteps, while at the same time embracing us with a hug of acceptance. Most of all, she is deeply committed to expressing her faith in the only way that really matters—through grace. Simply put, grace is a large moving object in her life, and you are about to be drawn in with a truckload of it. She understands that grace is never stationary and hopes you will take to the road with yours.

This is not a book with instructions for you. Rather, you will find in these pages an invitation to stop being a reservoir containing all of the good and undeserved gifts you have received or experienced but instead to start living like a large river filled with grace on the move.

In these pages that follow, Kim makes giving away grace look easy, because in the end, grace is not merely a feeling, like a ladybug landing on your nose; it is a decision. And Kim has decided to send a bunch of it our way. Buckle up. You are about to get a huge, grace-filled hug in these pages from someone who is awfully good at it. Let grace draw you in and pull you along.

Grace be with you,
Bob

INTRODUCTION

THIS BOOK WAS A TERRIBLE IDEA.

It sounded like the opposite of terrible when the thought first started rattling around, keeping me up at night when our house finally quieted down and a girl could think without the soundtrack of one husband, three teenagers, and a mini schnauzer who is wholly incapable of understanding his purpose in life if I'm out of the room. A book about grace seemed like a solid plan. Solid footing for earthquake days. Writing about grace would be a balm, a way for me to capture on paper what had given my heart roots over the years when everything else seemed portable or collapsible or flammable.

The study of grace has been for me a sort of dance, a swing of a pendulum that has dogged my heart and mind for years. During some seasons, I've felt like grace is as close as air is to my skin, as if the idea of grace is just as natural as August humidity in the cornfields of Iowa. But for other times in my life, grace has seemed like a melody sung in a language I cannot understand. Like a word I hear thrown around, particularly in church circles, but one that runs like sand through my eager fingers, faster than I can grasp it, smoother than my rough hands can tame.

Still, even with its wild nature, even with my inability to ever feel like I was really *getting* it, the idea of grace was one that just would not let me go. I couldn't seem to look away. This relationship with one word felt as beautiful as it was vexing.

Grace was curious to me, so I finally did what I do with curiosities in my life: I decided to write about it.

Rookie mistake.

There was a problem.

And the problem was the doinks.

Do you use this word? It's a very satisfying word to say. Try it right now. *Doink.* See? Use a little oomph with the consonants.

A doink is someone who irritates. Who clearly cannot figure out the best way to handle a situation or their mouth or their life, and this cluelessness drives us nuts.

I'm guessing you've had an interaction with a doink or two.

As soon as I decided to write a book about grace, really dig deep into the meaning and the living out of this mysterious, beauty-drenched, ancient word, the doinks were *everywhere.* It was like an invasion of the doinks. And the most disconcerting part was that the people who were the most grating and difficult and grace-defiant were not the people I had in mind when I started thinking about grace.

The pregnant woman at the intersection holding a cardboard sign? No brainer.

The guy who cut me off in traffic and mouthed "YOU ARE AN IDIOT" really slowly so I could catch every syllable? He must have had a rough childhood. Easy smile and maybe even a quick prayer if I'd just come from church.

The checkout lady at Target who snarled more than spoke? No problem. This has been a rough era for checkout ladies at Target. Drop a Starbucks card into her cranky hand and chalk it all up to grace in action.

It didn't take long for me to realize, though, that these moments were child's play, a kind of kindergarten-level grace. Felt good, not too tough on the intellect, and everyone got snacks and nap time.

But Advanced Placement grace? Graduate thesis grace? Grace 10.0? That meant I had to extend it to the people I already knew. *People I couldn't escape.*

People who waited with me in the carpool lane every day, knew my name, knew my kids' names, and who made it their part-time job to spread unkind rumors about us.

People who knew me well and had shared life with me for years but then dropped me like a bad habit when the world got prickly and conversation became an effort.

People who were picking on my friends.

People who used to *be* my friends.

People at my church.

People in my neighborhood.

Even some humdingers in my own family.

The doinks were everywhere, and I didn't want to think about them.

I wanted to think about quick grace. Random-act-of-kindness grace. Unmerited favor, sure, but I wanted to be the one to dole out both the merit and the favor.

And herein lies the rub that has needled us from the start. Really, truly amazing grace isn't a general gift. It's a specific one. It's a gift carved with our names in and through it, start to finish.

Grace is for the doinks that don't go away, the people of our everyday. God handcrafted it for the people who don't deserve unfettered gifts with no strings attached. God made it for people who can't afford the gift or the string.

God made it for me.

Even though I know it's the best thing for me and for the people around me, I find myself shrinking back from grace. It's the strangest thing, and I've done it throughout many long and rudderless seasons of my life. I've tried to earn my keep so that I don't need grace. I've tried to convince God that His offer is perfect for some but not for me. On more than a hundred occasions, I've gotten sucked into what Martin Luther called "the sin underneath all our sins," which is the willingness to gulp down the lie that we can't trust the love and grace of God and instead "must take matters into our own hands."

My hands are weary, and I'm guessing yours are too. We can't do this on our own. We can't crawl out of our broken relationships, our perpetually irritated hearts, our information-drenched minds, our badgered spirits, without indulgent washes of grace. Grace upon grace upon grace, to cover all the doinks in all the spaces, including the one sitting in your chair right this second.

I wanted to think about grace until I really thought about grace. Grace is big and wide and lush. It's what cushions hard drops to earth, and it's also what ferries us Home. "Grace" is an old word, an ancient word, and it's also so contemporary and relevant, the sound of it on my tongue makes my pulse quicken.

If you are in need of something rich and beautiful that you don't deserve, this book is for you.

If you are grasping for a reason to stick around and lean into the hard people in your life, the ones you can't escape, this book is for you.

If you've gotten sucked into thinking this impossible endeavor, the one that asks you to hold living and breathing grace close to yourself and also give it away with abandon, if that undertaking feels absolutely out of your reach, this book is for you.

If you've ever nodded politely to God's full rescue and then gone right back to striving, earning, digging deep, and doubling down to find the grace that sets you fully, completely free, I see you. I am you. I've been a very polite God-nodder. And the nodding has gotten me absolutely nowhere. My guess is that you're feeling a little stuck with that situation too. I'm asking you to put aside the stack of shabby gold stars for a moment, to take a breather from internal score keeping and spiritual tally marks and balance sheets you can't ever quite make work. Look this way for a moment because this book is for you.

Grace is for you. It is for me. It is for this moment.

And it's enough.

PART I

COMING TO TERMS

LET'S MARIA VON TRAPP THIS THING AND START AT the very beginning. What do we even mean when we talk about grace?

We use the word all the time.

We say grace before a meal.

We give people grace periods, and that's really swell of us, but pretty soon the grace periods run out.

We grace people with our presence when we are teenagers and realize everyone really needs our presence.

We shake our heads when folks fall from grace, but we are hungry to get back into good graces ourselves when the fall is our own.

When a word becomes this familiar, when it's slapped on decorative pillows at T.J.Maxx and has lived a robust life as a hashtag, perhaps we need to brush off the dust and define terms.

What is grace and why are our hearts so relentlessly hungry for it? Where do we go to find it? And are there doppelgängers to real grace, red herrings that lead us away rather than toward it? Will we know grace when we see it, or will this be a quest for the rest of our lives, until the bagpipes play the melody we've heard a million times but are still learning how to sing?

Let's start at the beginning. Let's nudge aside the clutter we've piled up around this idea and let's clear the space, take a closer look, hold things up to the light.

First questions first.

What is, truly, the grace that sets us free?

STAR FOR JESUS

GREW UP WANTING TO BE A STAR. NOT THAT KIND.
Not Kimmie K (though I do share her name) or Lady Gaga
(though I am also short). I definitely have a great story about
Gahgs,* as we like to call her around our house. I'll circle back.

I wanted to be an Exemplarette Star. Our church had separate girls and boys programming on Wednesday nights. This was
the early 1980s, a puzzling time in children's ministry, now that
we know better. The trend was to separate the sexes, for reasons
likely having to do with making out, drugs, and rock 'n' roll,
all things that were beyond our understanding in fourth grade,

---

* This particular story involves the singer meeting a friend of mine while
  Gahgs was wearing a variety of items, including a tutu and nipple Band-Aids.
  Confirmed: Lady Gaga is not from Iowa.

but whatever. We obeyed, and every Wednesday, my brother would head to the church basement for the Cavaliers, a kind of Jesus-themed Boy Scouts, where he would wear a khaki shirt with a kerchief looped nattily around his neck. Ryan learned how to tie knots and play tag. When he met me at the stairs at the end of the evening, his kerchief was wadded up in the pocket of his jeans, his hair matted down with sweat, cheeks flushed after time in the gym.

Exemplarettes had a different course of study. We read the Bible, memorized the Bible, and talked about the Bible. There was no sweating.

Cavaliers knew their knots.

We Exemplarettes knew God.

Even if you couldn't catch this distinction by our names (exemplars will always beat cavaliers in a spiritual throw-down), you would have picked up what we were laying down with one peek at our uniforms. No kerchiefs for the ladies. We Exemplarettes wore dresses or skirts sewn from patterns. Dresses are inherently more spiritual than neckwear.

Prior to my involvement with Exemplarettes, I had no idea this happened, this sewing from patterns. My single goal in life at that point was to acquire Jordache jeans and frosted lip gloss, a little pink with a lot of white.* Homemade dresses were not a part of this plan.

I remember asking Mom about this, and she got a little huffy.

"Of course I know how to sew," she said, lips pulled into a straight line. "Remember? I used to sew a lot of your clothes."

---

* Mary Kay made the best version of this. I am willing to fight anyone who disagrees. And I will wear my Exemplarettes uniform around my neck (doesn't fit the way it used to) in order to underscore my sincerity.

I narrowed my eyes at her. I remembered nothing of the sort. Clothes, obviously, came from malls. Like milk came from grocery stores, and mac and cheese came from a fluorescent orange powder. My mom went on to say that back when I was a baby and before we could afford things like pork chops and vacations, she made a lot of my clothes.

"All the girls of my generation learned how to sew," she said, sounding an awful lot like she was trying to convince me of something. I said nothing but looked at the swath of material in my hands, doubtful it would end up as anything but a toga. Mom sighed, pointed to the kitchen table, where I was to leave my paper bag of polyester, and went back to her Louis L'Amour paperback, muttering, "Mrs. Van Bergam would be horrified."

Every now and then, Mom spoke in grave terms about Mrs. Van Bergam, her junior high home ec teacher. The main thing to remember was that Mrs. Van Bergam was horrified. Always. Horrified about dust, horrified about Hamburger Helper, horrified about the pile of ironing that had remained static since my birth, and now, apparently horrified about sewing. Mrs. Van Bergam lived a life of disappointment.

Mom rallied, Mrs. Van B would have been bolstered to know, and I got my dress, which I wore to the Wednesday night meetings with a dash of lip gloss if my mom wasn't looking. One of the items on every Exemplarettes agenda was saying the pledges. Pledging was big with the Exemplarettes. We stood at the beginning of each meeting, Raindrops, Sunbeams, and Big Girl Exemplarettes, and with hands over our hearts, we pledged earnest allegiance to the United States flag (easy, did it at school too), the Christian flag (a little weirder because we never saw that thing anywhere else), and the Holy Bible (weirdest because was that even a thing?). As a firstborn child, I have an open affection for directions and list making, so I pretty much crushed this stuff. I pledged and recited and memorized like a beast, and then I waited with a smug smile for my prize. Prizes came from points we earned to spend in the Exemplarettes "store." I remember not one thing I scored with all my good-job-pledging-and-memorizing money, but I do remember wishing that whoever was doing the shopping for the Exemplarettes store would purchase fewer bookmarks with fuzzy-lens paintings of Jesus and instead allow the occasional bag of Now and Laters. Or at least a coupon for Mary Kay.

I'VE ALWAYS LOVED a clear path to victory. Sometimes I make one up if there isn't one readily available. For example, I used to force my brother to play "library" with me. These days, Ryan is over six feet tall and ripped, but there was a time that he was puny with a crop of blunt-cut blond bangs. The visuals encouraged me to feel the freedom to boss him around.

We would gather all the children's books on the hardwood floor of our shared room, and I would take out the red permanent marker that I would later associate with Liam Hellman, a classmate who would sniff that same brand to get buzzed during high school government class. I'd push the brick-red ink onto the pages of our books, lettering "K–I–M" at the tops of the title pages. The goal was to assign irreversible ownership to all our books and then slide them down the tiny play slide we had in our room, where they would crash into Ryan's hands. Ry's job was to gather the labeled books and stack them.

It was the absolute most unspectacular job. The kid didn't even get a single book out of it. I never wrote his name at the top of any page. That was not the goal. The goal was my own literary dominance.

I want to point out that Ryan still talks to me and is a really great brother, despite my efforts to squeeze all good character traits out of him.

I also want to point out that I had an early start making dumb goals and then running full-tilt after them. I did this in all sorts of ways and places, from academic pursuits to dating relationships to career thrashings to parenting. The goal wasn't really to live well; it was more to crush the steps I needed to crush in order to get to the next crush. The carrot moved a lot, but I just kept crushing.

Unfortunately, I got really good at it.

EVERY YEAR, THE Big Girl Exemplarettes went on a camp-out. This idea sent a shiver up every polyester uniform because "campout" sounded an awful lot like something a real, *secular* Girl Scout would do. Most were loath to admit it, but any Exemplarette who was honest with herself would have to say we had some serious Girl Scout envy. Hearty, plucky, braided, bad-a Girl Scouts. First, the cookies. Second, they were allowed to go outside into God's actual creation instead of just memorizing key verses of the Genesis narrative. And third, they learned how to build fires and weave baskets and identify poisonous mushrooms. Skills. Practical, real-life skills. Heck, they were probably sewing their own shapeless dresses from patterns even as we squirreled away points for another fuzzy Jesus paperweight.

By the time I'd made it to the age of eligibility for the campout, the hype was at a fever pitch. Sadly, we doomed it to underwhelm before we stepped foot onto the church bus. I only attended one of the two years I could have participated because the first hurrah told me all I needed to know.

I've always placed undue importance on food moments, I know. But Exemplarettes campout food was a grave disappointment. I'd suspected we wouldn't be grilling trout we caught for dinner, mostly because we didn't know how to fish or to identify a trout. Still, I was hoping for a burger or a hot dog. Maybe a s'more. For our campout dinner, we ate "hobo packs," foil-wrapped packets of carrots, potatoes, and ground beef. Salt, it turned out, was against campout rules. S'mores were a no. The singing around the campfire was okay, but I learned later that summer at YMCA camp that songs around a campfire are one thousand percent better if they are bawdy. Our Exemplarettes parent volunteer, a woman who had removed all her eyebrows and then penciled them back in with a skinny crayon, did not seem the bawdy type. She did seem very concerned about our rest, and we were all bedded down in our tents before the sun was down.

Faux Girl Scouts, all the way.

The campout wasn't a total loss, however, because it counted for points toward becoming a Star. Here are some other things one could do to rack up Star points:

1. Rake an elderly person's leaves. (Limited to fall, when most Exemplarettes were still just trying to get their moms to make their darn dresses, so the window of opportunity was small.)
2. Read the Bible.

Stars were required to read the entire Bible, cover to cover. Our blue three-ring binders listed every book, along with one little square corresponding to each chapter in each book. You might as well have put a quarter in me and watched me go. Nothing speaks to this girl like a line of empty boxes to check. I make boxes to check off items I have already completed, still to this middle-aged day. Boxes are my jam.

Not all boxes were created equal, though. Genesis had all sorts of inappropriate stuff, things that Eyebrow Lady at the campout likely did not read, so those fifty chapters went pretty quickly. Same for all the Jesus stories in the Gospels. Esther and Ruth had a couple things going for them. For one, the protagonists were women, which was a refreshing switch-up from all the old men in bathrobes. And two, they had love stories, which reminded me of my own unrequited crush on Darrin Jacobs, the boy with gray eyes and horrible penmanship in Mrs. Monroe's class who had stolen my heart. He was not very much like King Xerxes (not royal and no concubines) or Boaz (not rich or my distant relative, or at least I hoped not). Still, there was something in there that sounded a little like us.

Leviticus was more of a challenge. Pages upon pages of offerings and feasts, doves and goats to be sacrificed, things to eat (lamb and olive oil), things not to eat (shrimp and bacon), what to do about foreigners, periods, pregnancies, sexual intercourse, and all sorts of things that were big fat mumbo jumbo to me. I had a couple years to go before every comment at school was laced with clumsy innuendo, so all the sex stuff was clinical at best, disgusting at worst. No matter. I had a box to check. So I would sit on the floor of my bedroom, next to my waterbed, back against my ballet slipper wallpaper, and I would read Leviticus out loud so that the sound of my voice would keep me from sleep. Here's a warm-up from 11:29–33 (NLT) (I recommend reading it out loud, wherever you are, and just don't worry about the reactions of those around you):

> "Of the small animals that scurry or creep on the ground, these are unclean for you: the mole, the mouse, the great lizard of all varieties, the gecko, the monitor lizard, the common lizard, the sand lizard, and the chameleon. All of these small animals are unclean for you. If you touch the dead body of such an animal, you will be defiled until evening...If such an animal dies and falls into a clay pot, everything in the pot will be defiled, and the pot must be smashed."

Reading aloud didn't help me understand those words any better, but it did make me watch with wariness as my Cavalier brother poked at the carcass of his newly dead pet newt. Seemed a lot like one of the forbidden lizard situations to me.

Even if I was totally lost on the words in Leviticus, reading that chapter did allow me to check another box. Which allowed me to become a Star and wear a white dress and blue satin cape in a candlelit ceremony.

Bring on the lizard prohibitions and move out of my way.

☆ ☆ ☆

ALL THOSE CHAPTERS and verses, all those checked boxes, they sure took a circuitous route on their way to sinking into my actual heart. I'm positive my Exemplarettes leaders, my Sunday school teachers, my pastors, my parents all had a lot to say about grace. I'm also positive I have very selective hearing.

For a shocking number of years, I operated like God was extremely preoccupied with my checked boxes. I made up a compelling argument in my head that one of God's roles was to monitor my progress as I pulled on my starched Peter Pan collar, and that He would shake His head when I'd read the same sentence over and over and still didn't have a sweet clue what it meant. I probably heard the word "grace" the very night when I was six years old and decided I wanted what the pastor up front was talking about. I'd guess the pastor mentioned grace even as I said yes, I wanted to have Jesus take up residence in my little heart, to sweep out the corners and move in with freedom and life and always with Him.

But somewhere along the way, and I think the somewhere started real early, I got confused about my role in this relationship. I thought I should be *doing* something. Following rules. Making up more rules. Reading the Bible at a certain time of day, for a certain amount of time. Praying with words that would pretty much force God to do what I was asking. Working and working and pausing only to check on the boxes. Producing something showy at the very least, and something really mind-blowing if I could pull it off. I kept dragging myself around a dance floor, doing complicated choreography that wasn't even meant for me.

God wasn't looking for me to be a Star for Jesus. He didn't want my tap shoes. He just wanted me.

I spent so much time industriously trying to clean up my act before I approached him. Maybe you have tried the same approach, and maybe the two of us made God sigh a bit. I think He's patient with our faux-campout, our snoozy singalongs, our flavorless hobo packs that we choke down in the same way that we trudge through a Leviticus read-aloud. He's not going to kick us out for that version of faith, but I think it must frustrate Him at least a little. That kind of interaction with Him is awfully lackluster, awfully robotic.

It took me a long time, and I still have to shake myself to remember this some days, but what God offers us is much sweeter. The boxes can be checked or unchecked, because that's not even the point. The point is God's nonsensical love for us. It's a kind of love that would much prefer that we get silly and make the Eyebrow Lady nervous with some loud singing and wild vibrato than that we do all the right things and end up with a completed list that sits at the bottom of a box in my attic.

Here's a funny thing about boxes and homework assignments: The really good stuff often doesn't make it to a to-do list. I didn't write down any of the most important moments of my life, many of which will find their way into these pages. I didn't itemize meeting and falling in love with my gift of a husband, Marc. No list exists for birthing my three beautiful babies or miscarrying and mourning two more. I wouldn't even know how to make a list to show how I learned about the emptiness of perfectionism, the many ways I stiff-armed God when he was teaching me how to listen for His voice, the years I kept polishing that Star crown instead of getting to God as fast and as often as I could.

The good stuff is bigger than the list. It took me a long time to realize that God is too.

STAYING PUT

I ALMOST DIDN'T FALL IN LOVE WITH MARC. I BLAME myself entirely.

Marc and I met in college. We took some of the same classes, and we sang in a choir together. I don't actually remember the choir part, but Marc insists we were there, in the same place, three afternoons a week. I trust him because (a) he's Eagle-Scout-level honest and (b) I don't remember most of my life. I try really hard some days, but then someone comes into the room squawking about how they need new poster board *right now* for a presentation *due tomorrow* at *7:34 a.m.*, and I get distracted. It's easier to just ask Marc what happened.

Marc was smart and funny and uncomplicated. That last bit was the problem. Uncomplicated? I was more into men who were a little tortured, usually dealing with at least mild depression, and into poetry readings and Tori Amos.

Marc was not into Tori Amos. He was a physics major, which automatically excluded him from angst-ballads. He spent long hours in labs but he was also a dorm leader and knew an annoying percentage of the student body. As we became good friends and would meet for lunch or walk across campus together between classes, Marc said hello to everyone, and everyone said hello back, including professors and cafeteria workers. And members of his Ultimate Frisbee team.

Ultimate Frisbee is a real sport, in case you're reading this with a side-eye. I understand your wariness because, seriously. Competitive Frisbee? Sounds a bit shameful, like admitting you have a sticker collection and you like the scratch-and-sniff ones the very best of all.

I was very snooty about Ultimate Frisbee until Marc with his enthusiasm for life persuaded me to go watch his team play a game. It turns out, Ultimate is a lot like soccer, only with a plastic disk that hurtles toward you at speeds that could poke out an eyeball and probably a spleen. It's constant running, it requires some serious hand-eye, and I will never play it.

Marc played Ultimate. He torched Ultimate. His team was nationally ranked. After stomping on their competition, Marc and his teammates would head to the Mongolian Barbeque buffet after games and destroy the restaurant's profit margins while eating their weight in noodles and protein and MSG.

Marc was sporty and kind and funny and hardworking and knew all about math-y and science-y things and how the forces of the universe made things the way they are.

But please note: MARC OWNED AND FREQUENTLY WORE A TIGGER SWEATSHIRT. Forest green with a bounding, happy, orange Tigger on the front. Marc was not being ironic. He did not get his Tigger sweatshirt at Goodwill. He got it at the Disney store. Willingly. With American currency. Marc was not mocking the earnestness of Tigger. Marc *was* Tigger.

Obviously he was all wrong for me.

THIS IS SOMETHING of a pattern in my life, this pushing away from things that seem too good or sweet or uncomplicated to be true. I used to think this was just healthy skepticism. That I was nobody's fool. That if presented with something too effortless and beautiful to believe, then I wasn't going to be the poor sod who got sucked in and found out later it was all a mirage.

Free lunches don't exist, after all. Something is afoot if anybody tells you otherwise. You'll pay for what you get, all right. We all pay eventually. At the very least we'll have to sit through a four-hour time share presentation. Or we'll get the free lunch but will end up working as a dishwasher later in order to settle the bill.

By the time I met Marc, this system felt very natural to me. If something seemed too good to be true, there had to be a catch. If I hadn't earned it by sweat, tears, hard work, and some serious teeth-gritting, something lurked in the fine print. My understanding of how things worked did not jive with the idea of grace. Grace, bone-deep grace that wasn't just a word at church but instead a word that rescued me from myself, that kind of thing couldn't really exist. Good, sweet, uncomplicated grace couldn't be true because that wasn't how the rest of the world worked, right?

The world was broken and messy, so all things had to follow that rule, right?

Marc did not follow that rule.

Grace does not follow that rule.

God doesn't follow that rule.

Marc and I met when I was starting to suspect that one thing God really loves to break are my dumb rules. I was starting to suspect that he delighted in dismantling the boxes I'd built to contain Him. They were really pretty boxes with lots of fancy writing on the outside. There were bows. Ribbons. And they held the shape of everything I could easily understand.

I was starting to wonder, though, if my ability to fully understand something wasn't actually an indicator of how true it was. I was desperately trying to boss around my heart, my mind, and the God who made me, but I just kept ending up with shattered, pretty boxes and a hunger for something I couldn't yet name.

I WONDER IF this is a firstborn female thing. We are bossy, we firstborn females. Or at least all the ones I know fall under the bossy heading. Sometimes this bossiness translates to solid leadership, mind-blowing organization, the ability to leap tall buildings and problems in a single bound, all while keeping our hair teased. Many times, though, the bossiness is just bossy.

Both of my daughters are bossy. I mean this as a compliment, truly. They have spines and tenderness, which is the lethal combination for being world changers. Ana, our eldest, came out of the womb with a clear idea of who she was and what she wanted, and she has barely wavered.* One of the less fun parts of Ana's personality as an infant was that she would not swallow breast milk unless it had been pumped and was either still warm or reheated to the perfect temperature. It took me a while to figure this out. She would hang out in the prone position for hours, and I'd think she was drinking because the visual cues were solid.**

As is often the case, the visuals were not to be trusted. The child was not swallowing. She was in the correct geographical location for hours, and she was just freaking hanging out. Like I was a swim-up bar, and she was only there to show off her new bikini. I realized this when my mom and I took Ana in for her week-old checkup, and not only had she not gained weight after all those swim-ups, she had actually lost weight. I felt like a total failure. My one job that week had been to keep my daughter alive and make sure she was eating. I was no longer required to shower, brush my teeth, use my graduate degree, or think. All of those things were superfluous. I had my marching orders, and the orders were clear: Keep child alive by feeding her well.

Mom failure, and I was only a week in.

---

* Unless you count the brief stage in which Ana really wanted to be Asian. She thought the most beautiful people in the world are Asian, so her goal was to become one. I support the dreams of my children, but I could not deliver on this one. Alas, no amount of pining could change Ana's Dutch-Norwegian genetic makeup. When you come to my house, I'll show you a photo of Ana in a kimono. The girl was earnest.

** Also, I was clueless and new at motherhood and so bone-tired, she could have looked up and started speaking Mandarin (see previous footnote) and I would never have noticed.

The lactation consultant,* Dot, swooped in to help. She had a cramped office with semi-alive plants, a sign that worried me. Dot also had an impressive diastema, which is the dental word for space between the front teeth. The space was large enough to be distracting, but not as distracting as Dot's own formidable bosom. That sign I took as an encouragement. If anyone was going to teach me how to feed my child, Dot was almost preternaturally well qualified.

Dot took a plastic baby doll and shoved that thing into her chest in a way that certainly would have killed an actual child. She motioned for me to do the same with Ana.

"Don't be shy, now," she said as she asphyxiated the pretend baby. "You need to lead that child to drink. Show her how it's done."

Ana never agreed to this system, so I ended up being best friends with my pump. By the time we'd finished that season of our lives, I lit the pump on fire and spread its ashes around Dot's office. She hasn't noticed yet, but her plants are super healthy.

Here's something I've figured out: We get into trouble when we take a quick look at a situation, a person, a relationship, and we put all sorts of rickety faith in first impressions.

I thought Ana was doing what she was supposed to do.

I thought Dot would be able to solve my problems because of her, um, disposition and experience.

I thought Marc would be too chirpy and happy all the time, and that he wouldn't be able to connect with my snark and melancholy and distrust of Tigger.

I thought I knew best from what I knew first.

---

* Is this still a job? It was a job in 2002. Please report back.

I've missed out on lots of things and lots of good, growing relationships in my life because I assumed my vision was clear all the way through. I have walked past what God was ready to give or teach me because I just assumed I knew what was on the table and I didn't want it in its present condition. I have ignored some beautiful opportunities because they looked like they didn't fit, and I didn't want to put the time into trying them on.

Sometimes what we see is a big fat decoy of what's true and good and right in front of us.

I CAN'T EVER thank God enough for keeping Marc for me, even when I shot him down. A couple times.* The rejection we agree was the harshest occurred in my car, outside his dorm, where I was dropping him off after a quick trip into the city to hear some live jazz. Rain fell on the windshield, which made me moody and quiet, just the way I liked things at that point. If I could also have been smoking cloves and listening to Ani DiFranco, I would have been truly happy (but not shown that I was happy, because happiness was obnoxious). Marc might have agreed to DiFranco, but his dad was a cardiologist, so smoking was out. (Tigger.)

The rain fell on my Honda, and provided the soundtrack to my question that interrupted the companionable (OR SO I THOUGHT) silence.

Me: What are you thinking about?

---

* Marc says it was more than a couple times, but I'm the one who writes books.

Marc: (*shifts slightly in the passenger seat*) Actually (*clears throat*), I'm wondering how you would feel about me kissing you right now.

Well, crapola. This was very bad news. I'd had a feeling Marc was having feelings, but he was such a great guy *friend* and I really wanted him to stay that way.

Me: Wow. Um, no thank you. Let's not do that.

Marc: (*silent and really suddenly interested in the rain on the windshield*)

He got out of the car after a hasty goodbye and I drove around to the other side of campus, where I parked the car and trudged back to my dorm room in the rain.

Great, I thought. Just great. Now it's going to get weird. All our effortless conversations, all our laughing about the same nerd-o jokes, all our impulsive trips to go see a play or a concert or wander the city…that was down the drain for sure. I had met with some fragile egos in my short and broody life (I nursed one myself), and so I assumed that Marc would be understandably injured by my rejection and that we would have to resort to awkward nods when we passed each other on campus.

The next day, I saw Marc at lunch in the dining hall. His face lit up, he grinned, and he gestured with his lunch at an empty table, eyebrows raised.

I smiled back, headed over, and I'm pretty sure that was the day I started falling in love.

Who *was* this guy? This Tigger aficionado who bounced back from a shut-down and decided to just like me for whatever I could give him? Where was his injured pride? Where were his sulky looks and his avoidance at the beverage station?

Three weeks into finally dating Marc during our last year of college, I called my mom and said that I was going to marry him. Sometimes the best decisions are also the easiest ones.

I'm not sure there is anything more beautiful than the way Marc loved me when I slammed the door on his hopes and lips. He met me right in the little spot I was living, took a look around at my cynicism, my wariness, my insecurities, my dismissals, and he just stuck around. He loved me anyway.*

God loves us like that. He doesn't bully us into quicker growth. He doesn't roll his eyes when we have to learn the same lessons over and over again. He doesn't get hurt and sulky when we don't say the right thing, answer the right question, make the best choice.

God meets us right in the little space we inhabit today. He takes a look around at our mess, our heartache, our distrust of Him, our relentless need to control Him and everything He has made, and He just sticks around. He loves me anyway. He loves you anyway.

I almost missed out on Marc. If he'd responded like a normal person after my smackdown, I would have missed out on the best

---

* He was also super smart. He remembers going back to his room and thinking, "Kim is not a girl who will dig a guy who sulks. No sulking. If I have any chance, I need to play this right." How about *that*? Free advice to the boys who are loving strong and spirited girls: Be like Marc. Your chances go way, way up when she doesn't have to babysit your emotions. Also free advice: Sweatshirts with animated characters will slow your progress.

of men to build a life with, raise babies with, grow old with. But Marc knew how to keep moving toward who he loved, no matter the look on my face or the sting of my words. God keeps moving toward me, too, no matter how fancy I get with my footwork in the opposite direction. The best kind of love is stubborn and persuasive, just by staying put and waiting for us to catch on to the gift right in front of us.

OTTO AND LINA

HOPE NEEDS TO BE STURDY. I'VE SEEN LOTS OF versions of hope, and the thing I've noticed is that rickety hope doesn't do a girl much good.

I went to a college that has a really old and venerated choral tradition. Choral as in choirs of people singing. These days, "a choral tradition" sounds like something that should come free with your new Model T Ford. "A Pony Express tradition." "A smallpox tradition." "A proud hoop skirting tradition."

Choirs are big at St. Olaf College. St. Olaf is a liberal arts school just south of Minneapolis. The campus undulates with limestone buildings and red ivy and students in really unfortunate Norwegian sweaters. St. Olaf is not, I assure you, the place that Betty White references as her hometown in *Golden Girls*. It is also no relation to anyone living in Arendale. You are not the first to wonder these things.

I attribute Olaf's choral enthusiasm to the hearty, emotionally detached Scandinavians who founded the place. They were a cold people, first, because of their ethnic heritage and a long-held practice of denying one's personal feelings in lieu of repression and ludefisk. Ludefisk is codfish soaked in lye and served once a year in the school cafeteria on Visiting Alumni Day. It looks and tastes just as you would think. It is, in short, a puzzle filed under "Things That Keep Happening But Should Not." The founders were also cold because they hailed from Norway, a place where they endured entire months of not seeing the sun rise above the horizon line. These people traded one frigid land for another, eventually ending up in Minnesota.

Minnesota is very cold in the winter. We tried to make the most of it, like when we would go "traying" down the hill behind Old Main. We'd mount contraband cafeteria trays like sleds and fly down the hill, hoping not to hit a bump that could cause internal organ injury and trying to remember why we thought Minnesota was the place to go to college instead of, say, South Padre. Surely there was a school on South Padre. Traying helped for a moment, and I would try to cling to that unbound joy when I would trudge across campus the following morning, fully geared up head to toe, unable to blink because tiny icicles had formed in places I normally took for granted, places like my eyeballs and my nose hair.

I wore Gore-Tex and copious amounts of long underwear to deal with the cold, but I'm assuming the original "Oles," in the absence of Patagonia puffer coats, turned to singing and choir-ing and playing musical instruments to stay warm and not die in blizzards. I reference the instrumental crew here out of respect to my husband, who was a saxophone player in college. Marc was really good, actually, and sat first chair in all the fancy bands. However, he was still in band. And band during college, to everyone but the people playing in it, was seen as inherently super boring. No offense to the St. Olaf Band, which is a very fine ensemble. They play beautifully and all of their families really like going to their concerts. But the band was never going to be as cool as the choir. There was a pecking order of sexy, and sexy was big during college. The sexy people were in choir. This was a fixed point in the social strata. Bassoons would never cross that divide.

With the benefit of age and a distinctly different idea of what's sexy, I recognize that this is all absolutely ridiculous. Choirs are not sexy. Bands are not sexy, that's still true, but choirs aren't either. Tenors aren't (though they will loudly protest because they're tenors), sopranos certainly aren't. Okay, altos and basses can be sexy. And cellos are always sexy. Always. They are also not in bands, so they already start with a leg up.

I'll tell you what's sexy: a clean minivan. My friend Julie told me once that her husband, Kevin, cleaned her van without being asked. Cleaned the whole thing, she said, even the cupholders. Her eyes got wide at that part, and she repeated herself. "*Even the cupholders.*" And then she said with a slow, knowing nod, "Straight-up foreplay."

The absence of fruit-snack-sludge is sexy.

Choirs are not.

We didn't know that, though, so we just kept singing and applying lipstick that was far too dark for our age and adding in extra blush to cover up the fact that we hadn't seen the sun in five months.

The top choir at St. Olaf is called the St. Olaf Choir. I can't imagine there was a branding meeting that went into the naming decision, but here we are, a hundred years in, and the name is still completely correct. The St. Olaf Choir gets all the good stuff. Top billing at all the concerts, the toughest repertoire, and the best touring locales and experiences. Each January is an interim term at Olaf when students take just one class for the month. The choir takes its tour during January, and we went to the best places. One of my years, we went to Seattle, San Francisco, Portland, Pasadena, picking our way merrily along the gorgeous Pacific Northwest and down the coast. And another year we went to New Zealand and Australia for the month.

Marc can't talk about this without vitriol. He's still totally ticked. The band toured South Dakota. Southern Minnesota. If things got really crazy, they'd dip down to Omaha. One time I told Marc about staying with three of my good friends on the top floor of a downtown hotel in Vancouver. He left the room without speaking.

Choirs = Sexy.

For a physics major, he is slow to the uptake on real-life math.

We might have been touring warmer climes, but we took along with us a little bit of Minnesota each time we performed in our purple velvet choir robes. I am not making this up. Full-length, royal purple robes made out of lined velvet. Each robe weighed approximately eight thousand pounds. When's the last time you wore head-to-toe velvet? It's not a breathable fabric. I remember the weight of the tiny pleats resting on my shoulders.

It probably helped me focus my breath support or something, as long as I wasn't locking my knees and passing out.

For one choir stop in New Zealand, my friend Suzanne and I stayed with an older couple in a one-and-a-half story that looked like a gingerbread house. Dark brown trim, cut-out shutters, a sloped roof, and a lawn that looked like it had been hand-trimmed with scissors. Our hosts, Otto and Lina Muller, looked to be in their seventies, and I could tell upon meeting them that they didn't suffer fools or disorder. Lina was slight but strong. She kept a perfect house, and she was in perpetual motion. Her slacks (definitely slacks, not pants and heavenly-days-no-way to denim) and simple cotton blouse allowed her to fly around the house like a water bug at what appeared to be her average speed.

I remember seeing Lina's half smile, but Otto was a tougher nut to crack in that department. Perhaps it was the mustache. Otto's mustache was a lesson in precision. I could see individual, perfectly straight gray whiskers and knew they had submitted to Otto's authority and mustache pomade for many obedient years. Maybe smiling messed up the pomade.

Otto and Lina volunteered at their Lutheran church to host a couple of choir kids for an evening during our stop in their city. Suz and I were rooming buddies for the tour, which was effortless as we were also very close friends. To this day, I have not met anyone with a sharper wit than Suzanne. She was the perfect person with whom to share moments like the night a deranged cat flung itself at our closed bedroom door, in a predictable rhythm and with surprising fervor. Our stay with Otto and Lina fit nicely within that cannon of experiences.

After a dinner of something sensible and nutrient-dense, Otto asked us to follow him to the living room and sit down in front of the television.

"I vant you to vatch somezing," he said in his thick German? Austrian? accent.

The accent was German.

Otto wanted us to watch a propaganda film about Hitler.

The filmmaker and Otto were both super sure we'd all gotten it wrong and that Hitler was a swell guy. He led well, he fought well, he was nice to little old ladies, and those reports of six million Jews exterminated were grossly exaggerated. It was one million, max.

Suz and I inched closer and closer to each other on the stiff sofa. The blinds were drawn, the air was musty, and the narrator droned on, extolling the Nazis and the plan that was brilliantly executed by a few and completely misunderstood by most. Otto interjected at regular intervals, making sure we were understanding what really happened during the years of 1939 to 1945.

"Is this vat you are learning at your uniwersity?" he challenged, poking his finger in the still air of the room. "Are your professors telling you the truth?"

Suzanne pinched my leg.

I clung to Suz's elbow.

Lina flew water-bug-style along the back of the room, casting furtive glances at us and at the front door.

Otto stroked his mustache.

The whole thing was nuts.

Suz and I made our excuses and left for an early bedtime. The velvet robes were super heavy, and we were all tuckered out, we said. Ha ha! Velvet robes! *Gute Nacht!*

I was young and dumb when I visited Otto and Lina, and while it was a five-star story to tell on the tour bus the next morning, it took years for me to grab hold of what the Mullers could teach me. By the time Suz and I were guests in their home, more than fifty years had passed since the end of the war. And yet Otto and Lina were tragically, achingly stuck. Their feet were still planted in the concrete of 1939 Berlin, and not only were they unwilling to leave, they were madly sending postcards to the rest of us. *Wish you were here! Look at what you're missing! Book your tickets and get here as soon as you can!*

Otto and Lina were dead wrong. They had spent their entire adult lives holding fast to a narrative that was false, empty, and destructive. They had spent their precious, fleeting decades on the wrong team, cheering for a dead hope. Even after all the pain and devastation, they were still trying to convince others that evil was good, the loss was relative, that we just hadn't heard the whole, glorious story. The emptiness in that home belied its cheery exterior. There was nothing inside those gingerbread walls that could hold up their primal hope of two lives worth living.

HOPE NEEDS TO be sturdy. Rickety, gingerbread house hope does nobody any good. In fact, hope in anything less than the One who made us is hope that disappoints. Misplaced hope can even kill something that looks beautiful and alive on the outside but inside is rotting and lonely and sick.

The hope God gives is alive. It doesn't die. It doesn't have an expiration date. Fifty years is just the first drop in the bucket. It doesn't fade or wear through. In fact, it seems to get stronger the longer I hold on. The hope God gives me is the exact opposite of most of the stuff I've hoped in over the years. It's nothing like the dating relationship I was hoping would get healthy if I just kept willing it there. It's nothing like the dreams I've had that have rooted themselves entirely in what people will think of me, how they will applaud me, when I will convince people I'm worth their attention. It's nothing like the way I've worked myself into exhaustion, hoping I will finally earn enough gold stars and will finally be enough.

God hands me a different kind of hope. It's true down deep. It has muscles that can hold up under the weight I saddle it with every hour of every day. I've tested it over and over, and over and over this hope comes up the winner. It stands up to my dreams and failures and hunger for real things.

I didn't know, all those years ago when I was schlepping my purple robe around the world, that true hope is a lot like true grace. I was so thirsty for both, but I was not the one to manufacture either, despite my efforts. Otto and Lina were doing the same thing, really. That afternoon in New Zealand, there was a lot of mustering going on in the Mullers' stuffy gingerbread house. But there was also a lot of mustering going on in my own heart. I was working hard to build a life that felt like a good idea. I was a pro at telling God I trusted Him to give me hope that didn't run out and grace that saved me without a hitch, but I was also really good at turning around and lugging all my insecurities and savior complexes right back off the altar and trying again.

Otto and Lina had rewritten a war. I had rewritten the Victory.

No wonder those velvet robes felt so heavy.

I would hang out for many more years in the in-between, the mess of knowing I needed a hope that lasts but still plunking down a pile of coins on whatever carnival prize seemed promising. I needed many years to stop getting suckered into hope that ditches. Years to know that hope down deep doesn't leave us empty. It fills us up and buoys us onward. It stands up when everything else is falling and breaking and lackluster. It grows brighter and stands taller when the curtains are pulled back and the light streams in.

Real hope can only be found in the One who has won your freedom.

The war is over, and the news is in:

Real hope is alive.

COFFEE SNOB

RECENTLY STARTED DRINKING COFFEE AND I HAVE
a couple questions:

1. Why am I so slow to understand what's best for me?
2. How did I write eight novels while raising three
   young children but without understanding the role of
   espresso shots?

There are no satisfying answers to either of these questions.
Pre-Awakening (PA), I appreciated the smell of coffee, but not
the taste. In fact, one of the first bellwethers of early pregnancy
for me was when I would smell coffee and it would make me nau-
seous. So I liked the idea of coffee and the smell of coffee. I would

act like a poser sometimes and go to coffee shops but then get to the front of the line and drop the volume of my voice to order, in shame, "Hot tea, please."

I don't even understand PA me. Technically I was the same person, but mostly I just have compassion for PA Kim who didn't know what she was missing.

One day, when I had been through an emotional ringer and still had at least eight hours of daylight in which I would have to be speaking publicly, I ordered a coffee. I had to ask the woman in line next to me for help. What did it all mean, all those words on those signs? What was skinny (not me, for one), why were the cup sizes in Italian, and what in the name of the Lord was "a double shot"?

I took my first sip.

Angels descended.

PA Kim was dead.

I had a lot of catching up to do, so I just went straight to coffee snob. No pit stops at Folgers. I skipped all the polite introductions and camped out from the start with a daily cappuccino with whole milk, no sweeteners or syrups. And I fully, immediately embraced all the T-shirts and mugs and Instagram posts that tell people how coffee-ish I am. I understand these posts on a cellular level. I, too, refuse to function without coffee. I plan my day around it. I use it as a weapon and as an excuse for my iniquity.

My children hate it.

"I'm sorry," I say in my whiniest middle-aged woman voice. "I just can't. I haven't had my coffee."

(Hand held up in my best Karen impression:) "Coffee. Then life."

(Eyes rolled back into my head and look of rapture on my face:) "Is there anything–ANYTHING–better than microfoam?"

At first, my kids would congratulate me on finally becoming an adult.

Now they leave the room, shaking their heads (WHICH HAVE SURVIVED ANOTHER DAY BECAUSE OF COF-FEE) and muttering things like, "She is ridiculous" and "Addiction is real."

I can't hear them because coffee helps me become deaf to things that don't matter.

I have no regrets about going from zero coffee to the best coffee I can get my hands on, every day, amen. There was no on-ramp through subpar coffee. I was too old and arthritic for that. I went straight to the full monty, the whole daily enchilada, and no decaf, please. I want to respect you when we're done here.

I have a situation in my house now and we call the situation "the coffee bar." I installed extra outlets. Mess with my milk steamer and you might end up with fewer digits. Hand me a bag of stale beans and I will see through you to your soul. Because now I know what the real thing is. And when we meet up with the real thing, we can spot the fake stuff from miles away.

PEOPLE PEDDLE FAKE grace all the time. I've thought a lot about this, and I have a hypothesis that we just cannot believe that grace is an actual thing. It's too good to be true, and our grandpas always warned us that there was no such thing. Grace is awfully suspicious with its absent price tag, so we tend to want to spruce it up.

When I was a teenager, I knew some people at church who got real busy on the daily trying to help grace make more sense. Their primary focus was making up a bunch of dumb rules for a leadership role in youth group that they called the Few Crew. This was red flag number one. Jesus was distinctly grossed out by making the circle smaller, not bigger. Most of the times He got highly torked off were when fancy religious people made regular people feel like they couldn't crack the code, like they were not doing the right things to approach God. Jesus hated that kind of thing and often called the fancy people names.*

I had to sign a pink paper to be in the Few Crew. The paper said I couldn't watch particular movies or listen to particular songs. I had to be in church a lot and make sure other people knew I was there too. I had to not date anyone who couldn't go toe-to-toe with the Few Crew rules. And I couldn't go to school dances.

The list was weird. I signed it because I assumed the folks in charge knew how to make teenagers into super Christians. It seemed reasonable that super Christians would have a really long list of do's and don'ts, and we all know how much I like to cuddle a good list. I was starting to take AP courses at school, and this sounded a lot like AP Jesus. Surely He expected a graduated scale of performance the longer you knew Him.

So I signed that pink paper and thought I was doing the right thing to get a high score on the AP exam. I also signed that paper

---

* A sampling: Brood of vipers. Dirty tombs filled with dead bodies. Hypocrites and liars. Dogs. Pigs. And fools, using the same word from which we derive "moron." The guy didn't come to play nice with fake-gracers.

because I was scared of being left out. I'd been a part of this group for years, and I was trying to ignore the weird in an effort to keep my place. Having a place feels good when you're fifteen. And when I was really barefaced and honest with myself, I knew I felt a particularly lecherous form of pride that I was asked to be in the Few Crew. Belonging feels good, even when we belong to the wrong team.

Teams are stupid.

When my mom got ahold of that pink paper, she was mad as a hornet. She saw it for what it was: a cheapening of grace. She spotted the whitewashed tombs from miles away. She could see past the claim that the Few Crew was all about leadership and saw it was really about pushing people out and making the ones who stayed dependent on their own goodness instead of the gift of the cross.

My mom, Patti, is super smart. She has mad skills flagging down grace imposters. And she typically takes them down with a single chin nod to Calvary.

"If Jesus said it was finished," she says, "we have no business disagreeing with Him."

She doesn't drink coffee, but other than that, I can't see any way the woman could be more of a marvel.

HERE'S THE TRUTH, according to Patti and according to God: Grace is real, all the way down to the bone. And we have no business adding to or subtracting from it. There is no on-ramp to the real grace because the grace we are offered at the start is the same we are offered at the end. Trying to make our experience of

God something that starts with Folgers and ends with a deluxe cappuccino, adding decorations and medals to earn the real stuff—that kind of thing is exactly what Jesus not-so-politely called moronic. We don't need any more morons for Jesus.

We don't need to sign pledges to clean ourselves up before approaching what one writer called a "throne of grace." When we pull that stunt, we dilute the work that's been finished on our behalf. I would never ask my kids to make sure they have their stuff together, best clothes on, and teeth flossed before we sit on the couch to talk. When my son Mitch asks me to go for coffee (now that I have seen the caffeinated light), I don't pause him with my finger in shush mode on his lips and then ask about the last time he cleaned out his backpack. Or organized his sock drawer. I go straight for my car keys. I just want to be with him. I just want to sit with him on a chilly Iowa morning, parked at the lake near our house, and watch the mist rise as the sun does too. I just want to listen to him tell me what's on his heart and mind as the minutes roll under us and the water changes color.

I just want him.

I just want us.

God is like that too. He just wants you, messy and broken and ticked off and confused and wondering. He wants *that* you, and He wants it before you can censor your words or clean up your act.

He hates pink paper contracts that add all sorts of words and dashes and commas to the work He has completed. He doesn't need our help. Our "help" just gets in the way of the good parts.

Once you've sunk your toes into grace, once you've had a taste of the real thing, you know the fake stuff when you see it.

You know if someone tells you to perform or to say something just right or do some sort of song and dance, that person is not talking about grace. They're talking about something else. And no matter how many bells and whistles they put on that thing, it's not the original. Put it down, walk away, and get back to the good stuff. Be a really nice snob about it. The other junk isn't even worth a taste.

WHEN ANA WAS little, she became obsessed with the *Titanic*. I blame Marc. He also went through a *Titanic* phase when he was younger. Apparently social events were at a trickle in South Dakota, and his mom was not about to let him play Dungeons & Dragons,* so he turned to researching maritime disasters instead. Therefore, when Ana started showing even a fledgling interest in the sinking, Marc was ready. The two of them cheered in nerdy delight when they heard that our local science center would be hosting a traveling *Titanic* exhibit, complete with actual artifacts recovered from the ship. On the first day of the exhibit, Marc strapped on his man-purse, Ana cinched the Velcro on her sneakers, and they happily skipped off to view the carnage. They did this three or four times the first weeks of the exhibit, and then it was my chance to take a turn as chaperone.

We made it exactly one placard in before I ruined everything. Ana, now the honorary docent after so many times through, pointed to a photo of the *Titanic*'s captain, a man named Edward

---

* I also don't allow my kids to play D&D. I am united with Focus on the Family on this point. No Dragon Lords at the Stuart house, thanks. We have enough to manage without lordships.

Smith. I read the text next to the photo and sighed. "Wow," I murmured. "Such courage to go down with the ship."

Ana whipped up her head. "What are you talking about?"

I shrugged, already moving to the next artifact. "He was so brave to stay with the *Titanic* as it sank. He died with honor."

Ana remained where she was, Velcro planted on the museum floor. "No," she said, drawing out the word. "No one died, silly. Everyone had lifeboats. There's one in the next room."

And here we have a minor difference in parenting styles. Apparently, Marc had been lying his face off as he walked through the *Titanic* exhibit, day after day. "Great news! Everyone made it!" "This sign says that everyone got a little chilly in the ocean for a bit but that they all found sweaters. Yay!" "And this newspaper clipping says that the best part was a joint sing-along on the upper decks to a song called 'My Heart Will Go On.' Fun!"

Ana had just begun to read a few words on her own, so she was none the wiser. It took a mother with no filter to shatter her dreams.

I cast no stones here. Marc was trying to do right by his daughter. Who wants to see a little girl with ginormous blue eyes and a bob cut have to face the truth that sometimes life doesn't work out like we want? Who wants to be the one to admit to their child that actually, the world is not that safe and not all stories end with giggles and ice cream? Who wants to be the parent to break the news that people don't start and end with a fair shake, and that we don't do a very good job of making space in the lifeboat?

Ana cried her way through the exhibit, and I have permanently abdicated the parental responsibility of taking children to the science center. I don't even like science centers. Let the physics major shoulder the atoms and the wrap-an-egg-and-drop-it and the water table! I'll be in the bookstore reading a novel, dang it!*

Maybe you suspect you've been missing something. Maybe the faith story you've been told has always seemed a little incomplete, a little sketchy in the way it goes only so far and then boomerangs right back to you. Maybe you've seen the pink papers asking you to sign on to behavior management and attendance taking, just so you can prove that you are choosing Jesus in real time and helping Him help you. Maybe you've failed miserably at this performance and you feel like God has to be close to cutting you off, considering all you've done and not done. Maybe you, like the apostle Paul, have come to the hair-tearing moments where you've shaken your fist and demanded of the universe, "Who will rescue me from this body of death?"

Maybe you've taken stock and decided that the ship is definitely going down and there is no lifeboat in sight.

There's a really great plot twist here: God isn't into halfway. He's a full-send kind of God. He's not into going Dutch on the bill—you pay half, He pays half. He's not into almost.

He's into fullness.

He's into wholeness.

He's into enough-ness.

There is room in the lifeboat because He IS the lifeboat. You don't have to keep swimming alongside, letting Him know that you're great! Nothing to see here! Just getting ready for the

---

* Another by-product of this event: Ana reads every single word of every single museum placard. Every one. Every. One. We left her in the Smithsonian a few years ago, and she's still making her way through the First Ladies exhibit. I think she'll call by Christmas.

sing-along! Use that spot for another more deserving! The spot is for *you*. Spots abound, in fact. No need to throw an elbow.

And once you finally take that hand offered to you, once you let yourself rest, covered in a blanket of grace warm enough to save your actual life, well. You won't ever be able to bear the taste of the fake stuff again. You'll start scanning the water for other swimmers who are tuckered out, alternating with the back float just to get to shore. You'll start waving like a maniac, shouting that there's something better and that all they have to do is give in and take the hand that can scoop us out of the cold and the dark and offer us a place in the warmth and the light.

No need to go down with the ship. That ship isn't worth saving. The real stuff is just a reach away. Hold fast.

WHAT IT'S NOT

DURING THE SUMMER, WE SPEND LOTS OF TIME AT a lake in northern Iowa. My kids are the fourth generation in our family to spend languid days in those waters, swimming, fishing, boating, making entirely unnecessary trips to get nutty bars. Nutty bars are a local delight, squares of rich vanilla ice cream dipped in chocolate and coated with chopped peanuts. They taste like summer, and we shame any visitor who doesn't lose their mind over their simple brilliance.

One hot weekend a few years back, I broke out in a rash on my face, neck, and arms. I went from ignoring the passage of hours while lying on a dock, a glass of iced lemonade sweating in my hand, one toe in the waves as I read my favorite book, to looking like a scowling Oompa Loompa. The rash was red and angry and quickly becoming something even a nutty bar couldn't fix.

The doctor at the urgent care clinic furrowed his brow and made his eyes squinty as he took a look at my skin. He kept his hands folded behind his back as he peered at the bumps and swells.

"Hmph," he said before putting up one finger and backing out of the room. The clock on the wall ticked long enough, I worried he'd gotten sidetracked by a dismembered water skier. When he finally returned, he was hefting a book that could have doubled as a compact car.

He shook his head, grief on his face. "I'm sorry," he said. He pointed to the open page, showing me a Latin word with eighteen syllables. "What you have is very rare, and there is no cure."

"Really?" I gulped, my hand instinctively flying to the bumps on my neck.

"I'm afraid so," the doctor said, shaking his head. "You'll struggle with this your whole life. It will come and go, but there's nothing you can do. And nothing we can do to help."

The lake has a million resplendent things, but one of them is not urgent care. I called my dermatologist in my hometown once I got back to the cabin. After I told him the Latin bit and we went a few rounds of "Wait, *where* are you?," he offered a different diagnosis.

"Sounds like you ate something weird. You have hives. I'll call in steroids and they'll be gone within a few days."

Sometimes the most important thing to know is what a thing *isn't*.

✩ ✩ ✩

HERE ARE SOME things grace is not:

Grace is not a weapon.

Grace is not a convenient excuse for injustice.

Grace doesn't provide cover for abusers who claim it as a no-fly zone.

Grace, like all good words God gives, can be warped into a meaning God never gave.

I knew a woman once who endured abuse at the hands of a person who said he loved God. He even said he would help her know God better. He was in a position of leadership at her church, so of course she assumed he was the representative of good things, right things, things that would buoy her heart and soul and body.

This man betrayed all of that and abused her for years. He told her he loved her, he told her he would leave his family for her, and he told her that she needed to have grace for him as he worked out the details.

When the abuse became public, the church leadership used the word "grace" a lot when they talked about the guy. They didn't say much about the girl at all. Her story hurt to face, and instead of looking at the pain directly in the eye, the people in charge said they were sorry, but everyone really needed to focus on grace so that everyone could heal.

Nobody heals when the diagnosis is off.

The pain isn't incurable. It won't define us for the rest of our lives. But we need to look at our stories and our wounds with clear eyes and strong spirits if we're ever going to get well.

If you have been asked to ignore injustice or abuse or racism or manipulation and to stamp that file with a flickering neon sign that says GRACE, I'm here to tell you the diagnosis was off. Grace steps right into the ugly. It faces it head-on, no wincing, no backing out of the room with a question mark on its face. Grace offers us truth and freedom, and if people are using the word or idea to promote anything with shackles, they are dead wrong. They are distorting a precious and beautiful gift, tailor-made for healing, exquisitely and expensively crafted just for you.

Grace does not kill, steal, or destroy, all to make somebody else feel better. If the definition of grace you've seen looks like that, run away. I'd shout a bit on my way out, if I were you. Once more for the people in the back, while you're at it. Grace doesn't mean we watch injustice and pain and nod silently, maybe say a prayer, hope everything turns out all right. No, grace is a warrior. It flips the lights on, not off. It faces the broken and keeps its gaze fixed on the One who sees all and loves with ferocity and truth.

Sometimes we need to know what a thing is not so we can see what it truly is. Grace is not an all-access pass to hurt others.

Beware of cheap substitutes.

MY FRIEND NICK has a strange tic when he says the word "grace." He makes a face and the tone of his voice gets a little gravelly.

"Grace," he says, letting the vowel linger a bit between hard consonants. Nick says "grace" like a cuss word. We are careful not to ask him to "say grace" before we eat a meal because we don't want him to spit on our food.

Nick associates the word "grace" with his sister, Ivy. Ivy was married to a guy for twelve years, and every one of those years was ghastly. She knew on her wedding night that she had made a horrible mistake in marrying this man. He was unkind, unfaithful, untrue. He used her body on Saturdays and showed up in a clean shirt for church on Sunday. He cheated on her with real and imagined women.

It's not that he didn't say he was sorry sometimes. He did. He just never did anything about it. His actions never followed through on his sometimes-teary promises. Ivy did what she thought she was supposed to do. She forgave him, she stayed with him, sometimes through violence and belittling, always with a sincere hope that her pastor was right, that the guy would change and that by showing him "grace," she would be the one to make it happen.

Nick wanted Ivy to leave the first time she told him, not even a year into the marriage, that she had not actually become super clumsy and that the bruise wasn't actually from tripping. Nick hadn't let up for weeks, volleying a parade of questions and becoming more and more bothered by his sister's strange explanations. Ivy had run track on a Division I college scholarship. She was pretty good on her feet. Yet the bruises continued, and Nick wouldn't let it go. And when Ivy finally told her brother what was really going down behind her front door, he wanted to get her out that night.

That night stretched to another night. And then another. And then month after month, and then to twelve years. Ivy kept saying she was doing okay. She said it would all be okay. She said her husband was just very broken, but that she and her pastor had a plan and were working the plan. The plan was that she needed to keep showing the guy grace. She could handle the pain and the setbacks, she'd say. Grace would win the day.

I wish Nick didn't tether this mutilation of the word "grace" to the one I know in my bones. I wish Nick and Ivy and Ivy's husband knew the true, undefiled meaning of grace. I wish they heard "grace" and instead of picturing a prison, they pictured chains falling and doors opening and freedom flooding.

I feel equal parts sorrow and rage when I think of the bastardization of this precious word. If the idea of unmerited kindness has come to take on a sinister gleam to you, hear me loudly through the miles between us: There is no sinister "grace." There is no manipulative "grace." There is no real grace in the way people pushed that word into your tender bruises, both the ones you could see and the ones you could hide. If there is someone in your life who used the sacred concept of grace as a way to keep you quiet or malleable or aching, that someone did wrong by you. That was not the grace that saves and redeems and restores. It's not the grace that plucked my own feet out of the muck and continues to show me something far better than anything I'd imagined for myself.

Real grace doesn't live in the shadows, and it doesn't ask you to live there either. Real grace breaks the locks and pulls the doors off its hinges, takes your hand, and tells you to walk, steadfast, into the light.

☆ ☆ ☆

BECAUSE GRACE BREATHES freedom into our lungs, we don't have to wait for the person who hurt us to decide they were wrong. I wasted a lot of years waiting for decisions like those. I had a serious, inescapable hunger for a few apologies. I was entirely right to expect the apologies, I want you to know. My guess is that I'm not the only one in this position. My guess is that you have a similar, absolutely justifiable list of apologies owed. People can be horrible. Sometimes those people are super close to us, in our homes, our workplaces, our families, our churches. We want them to move and they persist in staying right where they are. We want them to stay and they hightail it out the door, often when we're midsentence. Sometimes it feels like these people must be completely and utterly blind to their own roles as Pain Ninjas.

Their problem becomes our problem when we wait for them to own up. But here's what I'm learning: We don't need to lug around the heavy reference book that lists every way we have been wronged. That kind of life is too unwieldy. That kind of life punishes me, while the person who wrote a big chunk of those entries is blissfully ignorant.

Living a life infused with grace does not mean we skip past the pain. When we decide to let grace be the heartbeat of our lives, we don't move to Disneyland.* We don't paint everything in sparkle paint and count off four beats for choreography. We don't nail together a slipshod coffin full of nasty, dead things and say the Grace Police have stopped by and found everything as it's supposed to be.

Living into grace means we see the coffin and we look at it with open eyes, hearts, and hands. Grace helps us know what's

---

* Thank goodness.

ours to pick up and what's ours to lay down. We can look at the pain and dysfunction, the betrayal and the dismantling, and we can see it all for what it is. See ourselves for who we are. It means that we look at the mess, sit with it, process it, talk with Jesus nonstop about it, get professional help with it, and let grace lead us Home.

MY HIVES CLEARED up after a few days. Doc Number Two was spot on. He also cussed a little on the phone, so that helped me feel better pretty much instantly. This was an issue of incompetence, not a total loss of health for the rest of my life. I had been listening to the wrong expert, that's all.

Be careful with who gets to define grace in your life. If the definition jives with wholeness, healing, and a life bursting with abundance, you're on the right track. If it wears blinders to protect the tap dance of abuse, manipulation, or arrogance, sprint in the opposite direction. Jesus had no part of that, and you don't need to either.

Jesus came so you could dunk your entire self in the river of grace.

Jesus came so you could be free.

Jesus came for you to be complete.

Jesus came so you could join Him in making all things new, you walking next to Him, running, giddy, next to Him, grateful and marveling at His expert diagnosis.

PART II

NAME CALLING

WE TOOK A TRIP TO ENGLAND A FEW YEARS AGO. The airlines got confused for a sec and priced flights out of Iowa as if we were living on the Newark tarmac and could just jump onto a wing. We snapped up those tickets before the air people figured out their mistake, and we made our way with our children to the place where everyone sounds reliable just because of their accents.

I learned a bunch of new words while I was in England, and my favorite was "bespoke." The word refers to something that is custom-made, often an item of clothing that's purchased before it's created. Apparently the whole idea of custom-creation is having a moment after a long spell where cookie-cutter was the only way to go. The idea of having something made just for you sounds exotic and luxurious, probably because it is. Target, for example, is really fantastic and utterly affordable for the first ten minutes before my greed overcomes me. But I also know that the cute sneakers I bought there last week will be on the feet of a quadrillion other people by the end of the month. The sneakers are not bespoke.

Grace is bespoke. It's custom made for us. It's luxurious in its personalization. Grace bears our individual names, and it comes to us in ways and moments and whispers and shouts that we uniquely understand.

When we start paying attention to grace, one of the most beautiful by-products is a fresh glimpse of who we really are, how we, too, are custom-made. Grace helps us see who we were before life beat up on us. It helps us believe what God really thinks of us in His actual heart instead of all the lines we've been prompting Him with from the wings. Grace makes us start to wonder if all the hustle and striving we've dedicated to figuring out who we are has given us nothing in return, if what we really needed was a new look at an old word, a gift that was purchased at an extravagant price and that helps us see ourselves clearly, maybe for the very first time.

SPEAK MY
LANGUAGE

WHEN I WAS TWO YEARS OLD, MY NEIGHBOR RAN over me with her convertible.

This was the 1970s, and cars were heavy. The car was not a Prius. It was big and clunky, and I should have seen it coming down the sloped driveway, but I didn't. I was little, so I wasn't quite as verbal as I am now. These days, my family is well aware of my plans, because if I don't say that stuff out loud, people don't eat and they get left at lacrosse practice. These days, I announce my intentions, because otherwise, no one realizes that I'm on a work trip until I've been gone for twelve hours and everyone needs clean socks and all the lights are still off at ten p.m. and also the dog has died.*

Things are different now, but when I was two, I didn't make any announcements before leaving the room.

My parents assume now that, on that sunny afternoon in September, I snuck out of the backyard, where my mom had just left me moments before to greet my dad on his lunch break. They think I headed next door to pet our neighbor's basset hound, Hugo. And when Kathy, Hugo's owner, felt her car go up, then down, her heart sank to think she had just driven over her dog.

Instead, the tire had passed over my head, leaving its tracks on my soft, two-year-old skin. My parents heard Kathy screaming, and when they ran onto our front porch, they saw her crouching next to her car. My little body lay motionless underneath, blond hair splayed out on the pavement.

My dad lifted me gently from the driveway, placed me in my mom's arms, and we raced to the hospital. This part of the story strikes me, now that I'm older and wiser and have taken biology finals. My dad is a dentist. He knows a lot about head and neck anatomy. He knows to never, ever move the victim of a head injury.

He's also my dad.

He couldn't wait for an ambulance.

He's my dad, so he was ready to move any mountain that dared stand in the way of his little girl and the help she needed. Even if that meant breaking every rule.

---

* Incidentally, Marc also has access to the family calendar, but at the time of this writing, no one has ever asked him a single question about it. Ever.

I still have the little shirt I was wearing that day. The doctors cut it off me, right up the middle of the polyester print of zoo animals. The x-ray showed a bilateral skull fracture. My skull was broken in two places. My young parents heard all the things we never want to hear about our children: *Her mind might never be the same. She might lose her sight. Her hearing. Her ability to walk or talk or feed herself. We might need to drill holes into her skull to relieve the swelling in her brain.*

It sounds impossible to do, but prepare yourselves.

She might not make it.

Funny word, "might." It can feel so desperate, can't it? So reckless. "Might" means we have very little control over the next sentence. "Might" feels unsteady, shaky, unpredictable, like walking on stilts or moonwalking across a tightrope. Will it or won't it? Are we okay or aren't we? Just tell me either way so I can carry on.

My dad doesn't thrive with "might." He prefers, "See you at five." He likes, "The weather at the lake is perfect and won't change for the next week and a half." And, "This will only take fifteen minutes." "Might" is not his mojo.

In fact, two weeks prior to my accident, Dad had prayed a rather bold prayer that beautifully showcased his allergy to "might." He'd grown up going to church but really wasn't getting much out of it. His life was getting busier and fuller, not less so, and he said as much to God.

His prayer in paraphrase: "Listen, if You're real, show me. Because if You're not, I'm going my separate way, and that way does not involve rotting in a pew each Sunday."

Not a lot of finesse, but it sure was honest.

God had become just a little too "might" for Dad, and he was on his way out.

But then his two-year-old met up with a 2,000-pound cherry red convertible.

☆ ☆ ☆

SOME DAYS IT feels like we've forgotten how to talk with each other.

"With." That's the beautiful word in the middle of all those other just-okay words. "With" is what lowers the temperature in the room, helps us stay at the table for all of Thanksgiving instead of bolting sometime after the cranberry relish and before the pecan pie. "With" is what makes words a conversation instead of a Shakespearean monologue.

Talking "with" instead of talking "at" requires a patience we just don't care to cultivate. Patience is so lame. It's for things like gardening and origami and Dostoyevsky. See? Lame. It wears us out to be patient, so we just talk at each other instead, preferably in a room, virtual or brick and mortar, that's filled with a bunch of people who agree with us. Pass the pie.

The problem is that when we forget the "with," we miss out on some of the potent, firecracker, knock-your-ever-loving-socks-off stuff of legends. This stuff is absolutely free and available without a hitch. It will change your life, and once you've caught a glimpse, everything else feels like Milli Vanilli singing Sinatra.

The stuff is grace. Remember that old word? The old song that said it was amazing and sweet and saved a wretch like me?

We aren't really big into wretches these days. They're out there, of course, but they speak another language and believe toxic things and don't get invites to our parties.

What if, though, the party has gotten unnecessarily small? The kind that has lukewarm tater tots and ran out of ice hours ago and now has Kenny G on repeat because no one is taking the time to man the vinyl? What if we are missing out on the whirlwind, the fireworks, the richness that leaves us satisfied, because we'd prefer to talk at instead of with? What if grace is the language most native to our weary hearts, and we just need a refresher course to speak it fluently again?

I WAS IN Español Tres in high school when my dad, he of the "might" allergy, decided I was fully capable to serve as his interpreter on a medical mission trip. This was an absolutely faulty assumption. My dad was not of the era when foreign languages were a high school requirement, so he had no idea that Español Tres was a lot like Español Dos, which meant we were really good at saying, "The beer is cold!" and "Where's the bathroom? Hurry!" but not much else.

I did need one of those two phrases on our mission trips to Latin America. When it was all said and done, we made five journeys south, and I served as an inadequate dental interpreter for each trip. Even with my linguistic cluelessness, I loved these adventures. I loved the people we met. I loved helping in sweaty, confined rooms as we pulled teeth and filled cavities and did everything we could to help the folks who would line up outside our clinic at two in the morning, sleeping on their feet and hoping the next day would bring relief and comfort and a new toothbrush.

Sometimes my Spanish worked, and the feeling was straight-up exhilarating. My heart would pound and my grin would widen when something I'd learned in a textbook made actual, real-time sense in a conversation in the middle of Venezuela. Trip by trip, my confidence grew and I learned more in those weeks than in years of "*¡Me gustan los tacos! ¿Y tú?*" I started to feel like I was contributing instead of just the dentist's daughter who wielded a pack of gauze pretty well but wasn't much use otherwise.

There were more mishaps than successes when it came to second language acquisition. After traveling at least fifteen times now to Latin America and Spain, including a stint when Marc and I lived in Costa Rica, I am certain I have offended at least a quarter of a million people by butchering their language of origin. So I'm kind of an expert at language disasters, and I saw this played out by my traveling compatriots time and time again.

Like the poor family practice doctor from the East Coast who, instead of asking each of his patients their ages, accidentally asked how many anuses they possessed. Easy mistake.

And the nurse who got a little mixed up with her greetings and kept coming in and out of the waiting room, raising one hand and saying, "*¡Ocho!*" This is the Spanish word for "eight," not "hello." Patients kept muttering and looking for a number on their registration card. "Who the heck has eight?" Shrugs all around. Ocho Nurse, undeterred and smiling, would leave the room, only to repeat the process every few minutes.

Or the time when my parents visited me and Marc in Costa Rica and I went over to help Dad check out of his bed-and-breakfast. I approached just as he was brandishing a stack of American dollars he wanted to offer as a tip to his housekeeper. When he couldn't find her, he stood in front of the housekeeper's six-year-old daughter and said in broken Spanish what he thought meant "Where is your mom?" Dollars at eye level, he was instead saying, "Where are your boobies?"

It's both amazing and alarming how much one word can change the entire story, isn't it?

We had a lot of help along the way, lots of legit interpreters who would gently smooth over whatever massive social faux pas we'd just committed and get us back on track.

I think God does that with us. I think He's the master interpreter of well-intentioned idiocy. I think He's exceptionally good at speaking our heart language, with all its quirks and slang and wrong words and mumbled phrases. He knows how to cut through our pontificating and our distractions and changes of subject, and He just speaks the language our heart understands best. He does this, for example, when a nurse sounds like she's lost her faculties. He gets the heart behind the ocho. Or when two pasty Midwesterners try to patch up a botched interaction settling the bill at a tropical hotel. He sees the generosity behind the embarrassed waving of dollars and hands.

And when a young dentist with a pretty wife and a little girl of two demands proof of God's existence, God speaks back in that man's language in short, declarative sentences. He answers without a stutter, which is just how the young man understands best.

"Am I real? Yes. I am real. Watch this."

★ ★ ★

THOSE DOCTORS NEVER had to drill to relieve brain swelling. I turned to my mom after a day or so and said, "I want Mommy read me." She wept because those words were my toddler-speak, just as it had been on the blanket in the backyard before I'd toddled through the gate and around the corner.

The word "might" shifted jarringly, startlingly in a different direction. "Might" became "miracle."

I had no surgeries. The pressure in my skull never grew. I took no painkillers, not even Children's Tylenol.

I was out of the hospital in five days.

When I went for my single follow-up visit, the neurologist sat with his hands open, watching me play and giggle and chatter, and he shook his head, unable to find medical knowledge in a box that would contain what he was seeing.

As my dad says, "We are reporting it. Someday Jesus will explain it."

Tears always streak my dad's face when we tell this story. It's been more than forty years, and Dad's voice still breaks, yes, because his little girl was made well and we have no way to understand any of it apart from the goodness of God. But he also cries because God heard him and God answered him in a language tailor-made for my dad.

We have no great explanation of why this prayer, this moment, this lavish gift fell on our family in the way it did. We have plenty of examples of when God did not answer the way we asked, when He didn't leave the doctors dumbfounded or our hearts racing with the inexplicable victory. We don't know anything, really, about why God moved the way He did.

We just know to say it out loud.

We just know that the trajectory of my dad, his family, and now his grandchildren, falls under the legacy of a bold conversation between a young punk and a gracious God.

Grace doesn't make a lot of sense, until your ears perk up and hear your own heart's language as the one God is using to woo you to Himself. God speaks the language you can hear and He speaks it so that you turn toward His voice and can hear that the undercurrent of every word is His unfettered, unbound, can't-wait-for-the-ambulance love for you.

We are meant to love each other with that kind of love. We are built to hear each other and respond in a language tailor-made for the listener. And goodness, are we hungry for that kind of conversation. A conversation that grows up from the strong roots of grace. A conversation that sings in the native language of the heart right in front of us. Lots of those hearts are weary and broken. Some of them are insufferably rude. Most are limping toward the finish line and wondering if anyone can even hear what they are saying anymore.

We can hear what they're saying if we perk up our ears and remember the clarion call of grace. Just like my dad forty years ago, people are praying for grace. They might not have fancy words to start or end, no "Our Fathers" or "amens." But they are throwing out questions all the time, in words and other ways too. They're wondering if anyone is out there, wondering if it's a waste of time to ask. Their prayers might sound cranky. They might not have a lot of finesse in the delivery. Their language might be rough enough to make you wince.

But grace doesn't wince. Grace doesn't retreat until we have our "mights" and our fear and our bravado tucked away. Grace comes alongside us on the driveway, in the clinic, in the waiting, in the watching. Grace looks us straight in the eye and says our questions are really good questions and that the best place to start is exactly that kind of wondering. "Keep your eyes open," grace reminds us. "Listen for your native heart language. The One who made you is speaking that very language this very moment."

"Eyes wide open," grace says again. "Watch this."

WHAT'S IN A NAME?

IT TOOK THE BIRTH OF MY YOUNGEST CHILD TO expose that my extended family thinks I'm a total nutter. Here's how I know:

My mom called my grandma when Thea was born and relayed the news that Marc and I had welcomed another healthy baby girl into our family. Just under eight pounds, cobalt blue eyes, safe delivery. Mother and baby doing well.

Her name is Thea, Mom told Grandma. "It means 'gift of God,'" she said.

Happy sigh, deep breath, hallelujah, spread the word.

Later that week, the news trickled back that my uncle Doug had been a part of the phone tree. He'd walked into the room where my aunt Michele was sitting with their eight hundred dogs.

"I have good news and bad news," Doug said around his mug of coffee.

Michele raised one eyebrow.

"The good news is that Kim had a healthy baby girl."

Michele whooped, frightening the terriers. "What's the bad news?"

"The bad news," Doug said slowly, "is that she named her Chia."

Michele nodded, picked up her phone, and called everyone else in our family to report the good and the bad news. Healthy kid, regrettable name. Yes, Chia, as in pet. Yes, Kim has always marched to her own beat. Didn't she go through a folk music phase?

Not one of my relatives thought this was out of character for me. No one called to confirm. They had no trouble imagining me naming my child after something you sprinkle on a smoothie.

I AM AN AUTHOR. WORDS ARE MY JAM. NAMES ARE KIND OF BIG WITH ME.

I didn't send as many Christmas cards that year.

Thea, as it happens, truly is a gift from God. She lives up to her name. The real one.

Also, I now announce family updates via text.

☆ ☆ ☆

NAMES ARE BIG with God too. He knows yours. In fact, He writes your name all the time. On His hands, in His books, even in secret. One day you two will talk about it all. He knows your name, and He doesn't need refresher courses or name tags.

And here we have yet another example of how I am not a lot like God. I forget people's names all the time. Sometimes I even forget before I'm finished with our initial conversation. This is ridiculous and embarrassing.

Marc is worse. He remembers unhelpful things instead of names. For example, I'll ask about who he was chatting with down by the mailbox. New neighbor?

"Yes," he says with triumph. He met the new neighbor. "Super nice lady. Drives a 2012 Subaru Outback. Went to Kansas City last weekend and ate good BBQ."

"What's her name?"

Instantly crestfallen. "Um. Not sure. Mary? No. Lois? No, I don't think so. Zora? Maybe that's it..."

The next Tuesday I meet the new neighbor when we walk our dogs at the same time. I report back.

"Her name is Lauren."

"Ooh, I was so close!" Marc grins, pours more coffee into his Yeti to celebrate his steel trap.

I stare. "You thought her name was Zora."

"Two syllables!" he says, mug raised.

God doesn't forget. This is incomprehensible to us because we can't even remember Lauren-Zora. I meet Dan and three minutes later have to humble myself and say, "I'm so sorry. Please remind me of your name," as if I'm the prime minister of something and cannot possibly remember all the people I meet in a given afternoon.

God doesn't forget. In fact, God is nearly adamant in Scripture about His attention to names. Names are everywhere in the Bible, and many of them are mind-bendingly goofy. Dodo,

Gomer, Isbi-benob, and brothers Uz and Buz seem like good starting points. Start paging through, and you'll find lists of names. Throw a rock in any direction, and you'll find the names of warriors, tribal leaders, kings, and queens. You'll see the family names of Abraham, Moses, David, and Esther. Some of the characters show stripes of honesty (Job), loyalty (Ruth), endurance (Jeremiah), and generosity (Lydia). Others are complete nincompoops. Those lists are long. Those names show us what it looks like to be thick in the head (Balaam), what happens when we elevate sex to an importance it can't possibly support (Samson, David, Solomon, oodles of Corinthians), and what happens when a queen torments messengers of God (that was Jezebel, and she was eaten by dogs).

We know the names of these people. God knows the names of these people. We are not a charming but indistinct painting by Monet. He sees us as the individuals we are, and He knows every one of us by name.

What if we don't like our names? What if, hypothetically, our mothers had lapses in judgment and named us, say, Chia? What if our parents were celebrities, which poses great danger when the task of naming a child presents itself? Some recent eye-poppers in the famous-people circuit include Audio Science, Daisy Boo Pamela, and Diva Thin Muffin.* I'm sure all of these children will grow up to have the defined cheekbones and chiseled jawlines and questionable relationships with reality that we love so much in our celebs, but I also hope they live above and beyond their names. I want more for them than side-eyes at the DMV for all eternity.

---

* Because we women don't have enough mixed messages about body image. Be thin, but eat that muffin, diva.

One thing I have come to love about God is how He knows our names but isn't one bit limited by them. It's as if He says, "Sure, kid, I know you're Kim, but let's think of that as entry level. I have lots more to teach you about who you truly are." He did this a lot for the people in the Bible. The names given by their parents were perfectly serviceable, but God seems to delight in breaking open their small ideas of who they were into the wide, deep, spacious ideas He had for who they were becoming.

Abram means "exalted father," or the dad we love and admire, which was already a stretch considering Abram didn't have one solitary heir. But God renames him Abraham, which means "father of many." Old man, tired of old promises and dusty dreams, you who feel washed up and overlooked and all done: God names you the father of many, nations even, more than all the sand on all the shores.

Saul killed people. His job was to kill people. He was a hit man, all in the name of God and country. Jesus intervened, made his life infinitely more glorious and also a lot messier, and as a result, Saul started going by his less religious, more Roman name of Paul, which means "small, humble." Big man on campus? Put down your weapons and your ego and your place of honor at every social gathering. This might look like a demotion, but you're actually going to change the world. New name, new job, new heart.

Peter, my soul brother, my lippy compatriot, the one who always spoke first and procrastinated thinking until absolutely pressed, he started as Simon. Delicious irony, Simon means "listen." Listening wasn't this guy's strength, and neither were patience, forward thinking, loyalty, or courage. And yet Jesus gives him the name Peter or Cephas, which means "rock." Mr. Crumble Under Pressure? Yes, you. You are going to be steadfast, true, immovable. In fact, get ready, because you are ground-level-important in the building of this new-old, vibrant, upside-down kingdom of God.

You seem like a disappointment, Pete, but I'm only just starting my work in you. Hold on. You're about to find out who you truly are.

☆ ☆ ☆

I HAVE A friend who helps people escape slavery. This friend taught me (a) my life is very boring, and (b) people still live in slavery. A lot of people. And not just in places far away that we have to Google to make sure we spell things correctly. People live in slavery here. Spokane. Sioux City. Omaha. Odessa.

I didn't know.

My friend runs in very interesting circles. I'm sure he has days where he has to do laundry or take out the trash, but he also has days where he hangs out with people who run countries and people who need to go to jail for a very long time (sometimes those two groups look a lot alike) and people who have a lot of journalists following them around with cameras and rude questions every hour of every day.

Sometimes boring lives are just fine.

One time, my friend helped coordinate a meeting between an Influential and Oft-Photographed Person, whom I will call Rosa, and a group of survivors of human trafficking. Rosa was eager to enter into the world of people who had lived very different lives from her own, and she readily agreed to do whatever it took to make the survivors feel welcome. My friend had only one crucial suggestion.

"Call them by their given names," he said. "The first thing a trafficker does is to strip a person of his or her name and force them to answer to another of the trafficker's choosing. Forget who you were, traffickers demand. That person has no value and no longer exists."

Rosa opened her home and her hands and listened well to my friend and to the survivors who came to stand before her. She looked in their eyes, took their hands in hers, and said each of their names out loud. Their true names. The names that represented the before. The names that they had fought to reclaim.

"Welcome," she said, pausing after saying each name, letting the words settle in the air between them. "I see you. I honor you and all the parts of your story, starting from the beginning."

The survivors, warriors with names and courage and wounds and hard-earned ground reclaimed for freedom, stood before Rosa, spines straight and defiant, tears pooling and sometimes splashing over. Names spoken aloud over all the pain and the grief, calling across the chasm of years and suffering to knit together poverty with riches, dark corridors and alleys with soaring windows and rooms fit for royalty. When we hear our names spoken by those who truly see us, long-buried hope starts to stir. Dead dreams awaken to life, summoned by the murmur of resurrection.

MY FAVORITE NAME moment in the Bible happens at the empty tomb. Mary Magdalene is there, panicked, frantic. She can't find the body of her Lord, and she's losing it. She bumps into the gardener and peppers him with questions. *Where is He? Where can I find Him?* She's clutching burial ointments, precious oils that likely cost her dear. Her hands are shaking; the bottles feel heavy and slippery. I imagine she balanced them in her hands and knew she, too, was seconds away from breaking into a million pieces.

The dream was dead. Jesus was dead. Hope had taken one final, jagged breath, and the only thing left was a dark and bare room reserved for bones.

Just tell me where you've laid Him. I won't ask any questions. I won't involve you, even if you did something wrong. I just want to see Him one more time.

Please.

And then.

Jesus looks her in the eye and says one, sweet, intimate, wondrous word.

"Mary."

He spoke her name, and that was enough. She knew who was speaking. She knew that voice. She knew the One who had snatched her out of the clutches of fear and loneliness. She knew the voice of the One who rescued her mind, stitched back together the broken spaces in her soul, reminded her of her true worth, true heartbeat, true self.

She knew the cadence of the One who said her name.

And that one word set her world alight, made her drop to her knees to worship, and then to run, weeping a new kind of joy, a breath-caught river of tears. Mary heard that one word, her name spoken by the One she loved, and she left the empty tomb and her empty life and her empty heart behind.

That one word spoke a sermon. That one word declared all the truth she would need for the rest of her days.

One word said all is not lost.

It said that hope is living and breathing and racing far ahead of us.

It said love destroyed the grave. Forever isn't a fantasy; it's the dirt beneath our feet, and it starts right now.

That one word said that grace is real. God knows our name, and grace is real. If we ever get to wondering if defeat and silence and bones and graves are the places where we are doomed to hang out forever, we need to straighten our spines and listen. The One who crushed emptiness with His heel is calling our name.

Listen.

Let the world go quiet so you can hear what's true.

This is the sound that remains:

The God of grace is calling your name.

EXCLAMATION POINT

I'M GUESSING I'M NOT ALONE IN THIS, BUT THERE are photos of my life I'd just rather not peruse. For example, there were a couple years after I got all my adult teeth but didn't yet have braces, and photos of that time period are best left in, say, caves.* My dentist dad, of course, was quite attuned to my teeth, and he had his orthodontist friend slap metal on those babies when I was nine. Four years and a lot of violent tightening later, my smile was a different story. My dad was weepy with gratitude.

---

* Let the reader understand: The situation was dire. My aunt Michele once looked at my teeth pre-braces and said, "Good Lord. They look like they were shot in with a gun." I still talk to Michele, which proves I love Jesus.

In fact, just this weekend he texted me my school photo taken my sophomore year, white, straight smile in full glory and surrounded by an orb of a spiral perm. He wrote, "WE HAVE DR. MCGARVEY TO THANK FOR THIS." Yes. Thank you, Dr. McGarvey, my hair diffuser, and econo-sized Aqua Net.

I'd like most to erase photographic evidence from my freshman year of college. My hair, no longer curly and peppy, was the color of dirty water, and the ends of each strand were dry, uneven, and brittle. I have dark circles under my eyes. My smile seems forced, as if I was embarrassed by how well that smile had turned out after all. I'm usually wearing bulky jeans or bulky khakis or bulky flannel shirts. This was because I went to college in the early '90s. This was also because I was experimenting in starving myself.

Perfectionism gone awry can produce all sorts of wonky results. We need perfectionists. I want my brain surgeon to be a perfectionist, for example. A raging one. I'd prefer that the lead pilot on my next international flight be a devoted, color-codes-the-underwear-drawer perfectionist. Every person involved in building every building I'll ever hang out in? Come on in, all you perfection people! Electrician perfectionists, architect perfectionists, carbon-monoxide-measuring perfectionists—I want you on the team!

Turns out, perfectionism turned on oneself, particularly one's body, is even more toxic than CO_2. It steals and muddies and confuses and leaves a girl wondering why the goal is always just out of reach for the mere mortal. That first year of college, I ignored a lot of what my parents had modeled and taught about loving what God loves, including my own darn self. I was at the wrong college, but the problem wasn't the college. The problem was me. I'd decided I needed to fix me, and to do that, I needed to count and measure and monitor everything I was taking into my body. Doing that, I thought, would make me feel like I had control over this unruly road I was walking. Doing that, I thought, would offer me the freedom that seemed just out of reach.

Of course, I was wrong. One look at the photograph makes that clear.

I HELD OUT for years (*years*) of my children's campaigning for a dog. When a woman is neck-deep in cleaning up bodily experiences of newborns, then toddlers, then more newborns and more toddlers, a woman is tired. A woman takes stock of all the people who finally know how to wipe and look after their own nether regions, and a woman decides she wants a martini and a nap, *not* a dog.

I caved during a particularly long lapse in judgment,* and I surprised the kids by asking them to sit on the couch, close their eyes, and only open them when a black, wiggly puppy jumped on them and licked their faces with his little pink tongue. A tongue that would later eat raccoon feces and launder his own crotch, but this was the honeymoon period.

Scout is a boy but named after the heroine in *To Kill a Mockingbird* because I had a few demands and naming rights was one of them. After all, our children were not to be trusted with names. Ana, for example, was very vocal in her insistence that we

---

* I had to drive to Missouri, for crying out loud. Missouri is a state away, and I drove all the way there and back to get this dog. There was time to repent, and I just did not.

name her baby brother Captain Von Trapp Stuart, and when I said that might be a bit much, she paused and acquiesced. "Fine," she said. "How about just Captain?"

Right. So I was the namer, and I named him Scout. Scout thinks I walk on water. He knows he would perish within forty-eight hours if I skipped town, so he's correct in making me the object of his idolatry. Scout has other eccentricities. He thinks his collar is a part of his body. When I take it off to give him a bath, he flips out. He looks at it longingly, there on the counter, and I can almost hear him saying, "Please, dear Lord of mercy. Please make that part of my neck fall off that counter and back onto my body because I might bleed out, right here, next to the running water, which is also a concern."

We are higher on the food chain than Scout, but we sure don't act like it sometimes. There are things that I've put on, ideas that I've welcomed into my home and into my heart, untruths that I've accepted as their opposite, and I act like they are just a part of me. That if I were to let them go, I'd be in big, mortal trouble. Maybe I wouldn't even be me anymore.

Of course, I'm wrong to think that way. One look at what's true makes that clear.

A COUPLE OF years into our marriage, before babies, I remember a morning when I stood in front of the full-length mirror. I narrowed my eyes and took stock. Marc was watching me, I remember, not saying a word. I realize now how alarmed he must have been that this kind of self-assessment was so frequent and so brutal. I didn't pull that crap while we were dating. Even the dullest knife in the relationship drawer knows to keep some of her detritus hidden until after the deal is done and the rings are exchanged.

I stood in front of the mirror, pushing and pulling and sucking in and muttering about the parts I didn't love. Of course we all know now that this was particularly idiotic because I hadn't birthed even one thing yet. I didn't know that I would soon embark on a decades-long quest to remember the abs I was about to fork over to three squealing infants. I didn't know that the best way to spend my time that morning would have been to wear a bikini every place I went, including the grocery store, the public library, and Home Depot, because that bikini would look amazing on me. It was my right, nay, my responsibility, and I squandered it.

Anyway.

I remember Marc watching me for a moment and listening to my self-punishment, and then he cleared his throat.

"So, how will our daughters make sense of this?" He nodded toward my reflection. "They'll imitate you, right?" He said it gently, but the words fell hard and unwieldy on my chest. Hot tears came fast. The light was bright under that question, and I wanted to duck into a shadow to protect myself.

They would imitate me. Of course they would. Just like I'd imitated my mom when I was little, dabbing perfume on her neck and wrists before she went out to dinner with my dad. The way she knew how to make people laugh when they wanted to cry. The way she sat with her Bible every morning and ran her fingers along the soft, worn pages. I watched my mom and she taught me how to move through the world. I imitated her, and my daughters, if I was ever to get such gifts, would do the same with me.

At least twenty years have flown by since that morning in front of the mirror when Marc dragged into the light some ugly and dangerous things that I needed to examine. I've thought of that conversation so many times, and I've sincerely, imperfectly endeavored to extend the same wide-eyed wonder I have of my children's miraculous bodies to my own. Some entire years I have wasted by forgetting the wonder. God called the creation of my body "very good," and I have spent an embarrassing amount of time trying to renegotiate His terms. Other days, other years, though, I have remembered that the less I bargain with fear, the more I'm able to gather in grace, even grace for my own fickle self.

Fear was oxygen for my war with my body. The battle raged best when I fed it with regular doses of fear. I feared I wasn't good enough, not this version of myself. I needed to work, often feverishly, until the version matched what I'd arbitrarily decided was the ideal. I wasn't strong enough here, pretty enough there, fit enough here, small enough there. And that fight for faux-perfection bled into every other fissure too: my relationships, my lack of relationships, my grades, my achievement, even the time I spent trying to hear from God. Everything depended on me, but the problem was that hardly any of it obeyed me. And though I might not have had the words for it, I was scared. Fear ran the show in my head and heart, and my body became the one thing I thought I could manhandle into submission.

What saved me then and saves me now is that grace will not play nice with fear. It refuses to speak that dialect because that dialect is full of things that aren't true. The very nature of grace shouts from glorious rooftops that we are not in control. Nothing obeys us, and hallelujah for that anyway. We are not trustworthy when it comes to deciding when we are good enough. The price for grace is firm and immovable and paid in full. There's no good-enough about it.

There's an old song that I love. In one verse, there are a few lines that are pretty much a plea that God would bind our wandering hearts to Himself. I know that binding myself to myself is a losing game. I am not an accurate judge of my own worth. I inflate it one day and disparage it the next. I am easily confused by what is actually mine to hold and what's just a raggedy dog collar that isn't me at all but is instead some misguided addition that I'm lugging around. The only One who can see me clearly is the One who made me, took a step back to examine His work, and pronounced me not just a little good. Not just tolerable. Not just a functional way for me to walk through the world but not especially remarkable. No. He took in what He'd made, the result of His work and the high point of a really big workweek, and He was pleased. He said the end result, He said you and I, our sons, our daughters, were the exclamation points of His creation. He said we are *very* good.

Today I'm deciding to believe Him.

RAMBO

THE SUMMER BEFORE I STARTED HIGH SCHOOL, MY parents decided it was time to move. I'd attended a small Christian school since kindergarten, and my parents had some concerns. They were as follows:

1. The Christian school had no football team. (Dad)
2. The Christian school did not believe in dances. (Mom)
3. The Christian school did not have advanced classes for nerdy girls who weren't going to win any track scholarships, even in shot put. (Dad)
4. The public high school had something called a "show choir," and though we didn't really know what that

was, it sounded intriguing and like it involved sequins. (Mom)

Open enrollment to the show choir/football district wasn't an option, so we moved. Mom and Dad said they'd prayed about it and we were going to leave our home that we loved, the one that had the wide front porch with a swing where I had spent hundreds of hours reading and ignoring my siblings, and we were going to venture out into the unknown. We were a lot like Abraham and Sarah in the Bible, only my parents weren't ninety and we were just moving ten minutes north to another suburb. Also, my dad never lied to a king about my mom being his sister so that the king would feel the freedom to bed my mom but not kill my dad for free access.* Looking back, I guess the comparison to Abe and Sarah was a little thin, but we did feel like we were forging a new path.

When we arrived in suburban Canaan, I set right to work. First, I unloaded my books, stationery, and sticker collection. Second, I made my mom take me to the library STAT to get my new card. Though this new library was significantly smaller than the one near our old house, the change was a relief. It was at the old library that my mother had checked out The Book. The Book was actually titled *How to Teach Your Child about SEX*, and the *SEX* part was in arching, yellow letters that rose triumphant from a dark blue background. In short, The Book was trauma between two covers. I'd stood right next to Mom when the librarian

---

* If you have been under the impression that the Bible is a scrubbed-up story of a bunch of puritans, you need to read Genesis. Like, right now. Put down this book and go find a Bible. Just read the first book and get back to me.

looked over her glasses at me and simpered, "Ah. Looks like *someone* is going to have an important talk today."

If only I'd had my wits about me, I would have taken on a dismissive air, telling the librarian that (a) her lipstick was a tad bright, and (b) I did not need the "important talk" because I already knew what sex was. I'd told as much to my mom over and over, so much so that she felt the need to go check out The Book and walk me through specifics because knowledge is power and she didn't believe I had any idea what I was saying.

I was seven.

I had no idea what I was saying.

In fact, that particular talk ended with me in tears, running out of the room and wailing, "MY DAD WOULD NEVER DO THAT TO YOU."

The old library held difficult memories. Obviously I needed to leave that place and never come back. I was grateful for a new library where no one had any idea what I knew about anatomy and fallopian tubes and hair.

On the first day as a freshman at my new school, I wore a white sleeveless top and a pair of shorts striped white and Pepto-Bismol pink. I carried a matching purse. Picture this ensemble, if you will, entering into a large public high school, topped with aggressively teased bangs and frosted pink lip gloss. Another accessory that would have made sense would have been a sign around my neck that said, "I am a cloistered nun. Please stay back ten feet at all times." I was deliciously naïve in this new world of profanity and innuendo, so when the bus of boys from the reform school hung out their windows and leered as I began my walk home, I smiled and waved. Unfortunately, this elicited an eruption of talk and gestures so foul, even I understood the gist. I quickened my pace and, when I entered the kitchen twenty minutes later, told my mom my day was great, knowing that the reform boys part of the story would be best kept to myself and my pinstriped shorts.

I wasn't lying. I liked my new school. I liked the crowded hallways of people I didn't know yet. I liked the challenge of my classes. I liked the sweet junior boy named Brian who had a locker next to mine and helped me decipher my combination so I was at least a timely nun in an unfortunate outfit that first day.* I felt like we'd made the right choice, moving away and starting a new gig. Besides, Dad had put up a new porch swing, so the optimism coursing through my veins had a visual, and I felt sure everything was going to work out.

This feeling lasted two days.

Sunday night after the first week of school, we came home from church, rolling the minivan slowly into the driveway that still felt a little like someone else's. My parents were of the belief that if the church doors were open, our family was going to be there. Our church held services on both Sunday mornings and Sunday evenings, so that meant we would rouse ourselves from afternoon naps and try to resurrect flat hair and disgruntled attitudes and get our rears back in the pews only a few hours after we'd vacated them. I marvel at this now because I

---

* Brian ended up being one of my very favorite people in high school, and we are still dear friends. He has asked on multiple occasions if the love interests in my novels are really characters based on him. So far, no. But that first day of high school wins him far greater points. (HI, BRIAN! YOU ARE IN THIS BOOK!)

am fully incapacitated on Sunday nights. I don't want to cook, I don't want to talk to people, I don't want my children to notice I am in the same house because then they might ask me to go to Target to pick up black shorts for PE or googly eyeballs for a diorama they forgot was due Monday morning. If Marc suddenly got a wild hare that we should put on decent clothes again and go to church for a couple hours, I would likely start to gnash my teeth. I realize this would only encourage his efforts at evangelizing me, but I can be very scrappy when pressed, and I feel certain I would win.

I unfolded from the back seat and yanked open the sliding door to see a gaggle of freshmen boys riding their bikes to a stop in front of our house. They all said hello to my parents, who continued on into the house and left my little sister and me to talk with the dudes for a bit. I'm sure my parents were encouraged by this socializing. All nuns need friends, and I knew they were worried that my transition to a bigger, hedonistic public school would be rough on me. They were probably so pleased to see a bunch of clean-cut boys who already knew my name and wanted to swing by to talk.

A note here on sibling attendance: My sister, Lindsay, is eight years my junior. She was constantly tagging along to everything I did. Mostly, to my shame, I ignored her. I pretended she just wasn't there. Of course, the reminders were fairly constant since Lindsay was the most perfect-looking child ever to bust out of a womb. Mom loved to talk about Lindsay's "fine features," a counterpoint, I supposed, to my, um, less-fine ones? When we were out in public with Lindsay, strangers would stop us and ask if she was a child model. They usually used both words: "child model." She was not, in fact, a child model, but we lived in Iowa. Opportunities for child models were scarce. If we'd lived on a coast or something, I felt confident Linds and her startlingly blue eyes and fine features would be making enough bank to allow Dad to quit filling cavities and Mom to quit playing violin in the symphony.

Since she wasn't too busy child modeling, Lindsay mostly liked to find out what I was doing and either interject herself or spy on me. I usually didn't mind,* and Lindsay was a good sport about my lack of interest in any part of her life.

The absence of my brother in this scene isn't particularly notable because he had likely raced inside to either eat a hot dog or answer the phone. Answering the phone took a lot of Ryan's time. He was very social. He was also a super athlete and very good looking, so people called him a lot. He fit in his hot dog consumption between calls.

I don't remember much about what the bike boys said until a lanky kid with strawberry blond hair spoke up. He was draped on top of a bike that looked too small for him, and I remember him laughing and saying that another boy in the group wanted to have sexual relations with me.

The Book had covered this material. It did not use the word the boy was employing to describe the act. I might have just broken out of the nunnery, but even I was picking up what this kid was laying down.

---

* Except for the time a few years later when she spied on me and my boyfriend making out in my room and, after watching like a voyeur for many minutes longer than necessary, ran downstairs and tattled. Now that I write these words, I see the brilliance of my mother. I need to deploy the youngest of my children as a spy. I need to stop wasting my time being a vigilant parent when I have built-in staff.

"Right. Okay, guys," I said, rolling my eyes and starting for the front door. "See you tomorrow."

Lindsay scurried after me, her blond pixie cut bouncing on her shoulders as she jogged. We tugged open the front door, still not used to the new handle, which stuck a bit when pulled, and we pushed the door shut behind us. I rolled my eyes again. This was the second time in one week that I'd heard really crude propositions from really stupid boys. I decided I'd need to look for an upperclassman if I was going to make a go of dating during this developmental phase.

Settled on that point, I turned and saw my dad standing and staring at Linds.

"What happened?" he said. My dad is a very even-tempered man. When he growls instead of speaks, we notice.

"What? Nothing?" I said, shrugging. "Just dumb boys being dumb boys."

"What. Happened." The slowing of the speech was a concern, enough for my mom to hear and come around the corner, empty cardboard box in hand. Mom looked at me, looked at Linds, and narrowed her eyes. I followed her gaze.

"What did they say?" Dad said, no longer looking at me but directing his laser eyeballs at Lindsay. In her defense, Linds would eventually acquire impressive skills lying to my parents, but at age seven, she was still a work in progress. She crumbled.

"That boy said the f-word about Kim. He said he wanted to—"

"What's his name?" Dad redirected his questioning to me. Mom looked nervous.

"Dad, seriously, it is no big deal." I tried for my hostage-negotiation voice. These kids were doofuses, but they were popular doofuses. We did not want to tango, I was sure of it. I was brand-new at this school. The last thing I needed was whatever idea was percolating behind Dad's crazed stare.

"Tell me his name," Dad said, stepping past me and my sister, who was now crying and hiccupping and STILL looking like a child model. Life increased in its unfairness by the second.

I sighed. "It's Sparky."

That got Dad to stop. He pivoted toward me, one foot planted on the first porch step. Frowning, he said, "What's his real name?"

"That's his name. For real." I held up both hands in surrender. "I mean, I'm sure his parents gave him a normal name like John or Danny or something, but the only one I know is Sparky."

Dad didn't hear the last part. He was already covering the front yard in long strides.

Mom sighed.

Lindsay hiccupped.

We went back inside the house slowly. There was nothing to be done. Randy was on the loose.

☆ ☆ ☆

WHEN HE RETURNED an hour or so later, Dad gave a bullet point report. The story needed no embellishment.

- Starting on our block, Dad went door to door. Bang, bang, bang. "Hi, I'm your new neighbor. Do you know a kid named Sparky?" Mom had her head in her hands at this point, not just because I was crying as I listened to this recap, but also because she was wondering how they would bridge the gap from bang, bang, bang interrogation to a neighborhood Christmas open house she'd hoped to host. She'd even bought the decorative paper plates.*

- Three blocks in, Dad found my friend Tori at home. After my inaugural week of school, I knew two girls in my class. Tori was one of them. Tori knew Sparky. She gave my dad his address and likely wondered if all Christian school parents were this volatile. I noticed she never swore around me after this interaction.

- Dad did the bang, bang, bang thing at Sparky's apartment door. One of the bike riders opened the door, took one look at Crazy Randy, plucked the Nintendo controller out of Sparky's hand, and shoved him out the door. Dad asked if Sparky's own father was home, and Sparky said he was not. Dad put Sparky's lanky bod up against the wall, looked him in the eye, and said, "If you ever talk like that again in front of either of my daughters, I will personally come over here and rip your head off."

- Sparky agreed to the soundness of this plan.

- Dad came home to report and have a sandwich.

- I went to sleep crying. Public school was out. The only thing left was homeschooling, and even at fourteen, I knew I was not cut out for that gig.

The next morning, I came downstairs to get some breakfast before beginning the trudge to school. My mom says she felt

---

* We started using them for ordinary goulash dinners the following day.

relief flood her when I glanced at my dad, bent over his peanut butter toast, and said, "Morning, Rambo." In our family, that kind of greeting meant forgiveness. Dad looked a little circumspect, now that the adrenaline had run its course, but I knew he had zero regrets.

Summoning all of that zero-regrets-ness, I opened the door to the high school a half hour later. I have a vivid recollection of walking down the freshman hallway and seeing people part like the Red Sea, whispering behind their hands as I passed. It was a fully John Hughes moment, and I really did not want to be Molly Ringwald. I wanted to be a nameless, faceless extra, but my anonymity was collateral damage after Dad's hunting expedition.

Sparky's locker was just a few down from mine, and he watched me approach. A smattering of the bike crew stood around him. I noticed they looked nervous, as if I was going to shove them up against the bank of lockers too. As if wild paternal instincts were passed down genetically and I was about to spend the next four years pushing people up against the walls during passing periods.

I didn't stop to chat, but I did lift my chin in greeting. "Sparky."

He smirked for the benefit of his posse, but I saw a flicker of insecurity in his eyes. "Hey," he said, right before his best mate, Trent, blurted out, "Your dad is a bad***."

None of those boys ever asked me out. Not a one. In fact, it wasn't until my senior year of high school that any boy in my graduating class asked me out, and I think it happened only because that kid didn't know the Sparky story.

Also, Sparky moved out of state the following month. His posse blamed me, and I think they were only half kidding.

My dad is pretty sheepish about this story now. Twenty-five years later, his instincts have shifted more in the direction of diplomacy, less in the direction of Chuck Norris. For me, though, this story is pretty much perfect. I made it through high school, even with this notably rocky start, and do you know what stuck with me? Not trig or geometry or that really horrible self-esteem class or our history teacher who wore leather pants. Okay, maybe she stuck with me. I have never been tempted to buy leather in any piece of clothing. But do you know what remains a powerful undercurrent in the way I think about myself and my life and what I can do?

Rambo sticks with me.

I am loved by a Rambo. I am loved fiercely, loudly, assertively by a man who would ignore his own pride and self-interest and fledgling reputation in order to make very clear that the love of a father will efficiently and quickly tackle any mountain along her path. How dare that mountain stand in her way, especially if that mountain knows the f-word.

I think everybody wants to be loved like that. Everybody wants to be fought for. Treasured. Defended. We want to know that someone is going to come out swinging for us. We want to know we are not in this alone and that someone bigger and stronger and with a lot more pull is going to remind us of who we are, whose we are, and go door to door if necessary in order for us to believe it.

We want to be loved like that. And we are. You don't need Rambo Randy to be your dad. The One who hung ropes of stars and filled the oceans fought to the literal death for you. He won you. You're His. He gets to tell you who you really are, and He says you are stunning. You are beloved. You are His favorite part of a wild, free, matchless creation. You're the pinnacle.

You are His. His fight is for you.

MISTAKEN IDENTITY

WAS ON A BIKE RIDE WITH MY THREE KIDS WHEN MY agent called and delivered the news that I wasn't raunchy enough.

This wasn't a personal judgment; he was just the messenger.

I pulled over and took off my helmet to hear him more clearly. My kids looked at me, curious for about twenty seconds, and then started to pedal back and forth along the bike path while I stood with the phone pressed to my cheek.

"The editor at [important and powerful publishing house] really loves your manuscript. She loves the voice and the humor and the rom-com feel. Very Tom Hanks and Meg Ryan." I'd gotten used to my agent's voice when he was about to say something

I would hate. He was using that voice now. He sighed. "The terms of her offer are terrible. But! But! She said they could offer much more and sell a bunch of copies if you just do two things."

Here were the two things, in alphabetical order:

1. Rewrite my main character to have a lot of sex with a lot of people.
2. Write the sex scenes to be raunchy.

I said no to the offer. Well, first I cried for a week and said things like this to Marc:

- "It's taken me a decade to break into a house like this! If I don't accept this offer, I'll never get another chance!"

   (**Marc:** "That makes no sense. You are not a prophet. In fact, prophets tend to creep you out.")

- "This is so insulting! Do they think people will only read a romance if it's smutty? Whatever happened to the *chase*? The *chemistry*? The *banter*?"

   (**Marc:** "Very insulting. Also, I'm okay if you're a little smutty in real life.")

- "I was born in the wrong era! If I were wearing a poodle skirt right now, we wouldn't even be having this conversation!"

(**Marc,** wagging his eyebrows: "Wait. DO YOU HAVE A
POODLE SKIRT?")

The thing is, I was never really at home with any spot in
publishing. I'd written a passel of books for the Christian fiction
market, and each time I ended up feeling like I was pushing a
legalistic envelope stuffed with lots of weird rules. My characters were inescapably flawed. They employed irreverent humor
and felt pretty good about it. They made out with their husbands, they thought some church people acted like idiots, and
they drank wine on occasion. I'd had publishers say things like,
"It's fine if your character is, like, an alcoholic or something. But
no glass of wine with dinner. We don't want to glamorize sin."*
And "Let's not use the word 'shag,' or other flippant mentions of
intercourse."

(Note: It is never, ever a good moment when your middle-
aged, reserved, male publisher calls you on a Saturday and enun-
ciates with careful consonants *"intercourse."* It's an even worse
moment when you respond with this exclamation: "Phil, I am a
Christian and I like sex!" The relationship was never the same.)

So the Christians didn't really know what to do with me.

And here I was knocking on the door of the mainstream
market, and while no one was worried anymore about a character
doing shots of Fireball, they were definitely concerned that I was
Pollyanna. I was Lucille Ball seventy years too late. I was Laura
Blooming Ingalls.

Rodeo after rodeo, fretful editorial call after fretful editorial
call, I was gathering that it was going to take a pretty strong spine

---

* Don't tell that to all those revelers in Cana of Galilee!

to remember who I was and who I was not. And the truth started not just to emerge but to show up in blinking theater lights above every one of these conversations: YOU, KIMMY PANTS, WILL NEED TO BE THE ONLY ONE IN CHARGE OF REMEMBERING WHO YOU ARE.

☆ ☆ ☆

I FEEL LIKE I was a woefully slow study with this idea. Nineteen eighty-five, for example, would have been a better time to really bring this one home and let it sink in. That was the year I was in fourth grade, and that was the year that Helga Von Shertenplatz became my first brush with female friendship purgatory. Helga Von Shertenplatz is not her real name, but I want to speak freely and protect Helga, who has probably evolved into a very lovely person today. She probably tends to a windowsill of succulents. And feeds stray puppies. And plays the harpsichord.

In fourth grade, though, Helga was a piece of work. I couldn't figure her out. One day, we were besties and she would draw cute animated characters for me and slip them into my Trapper Keeper. The very next day she would whisper cruel comments about my clothes or roll her eyes at every word I said, as if my very presence made her weary.

When I arrived at the fourth-grade hallway one morning, I could feel eyes on me. I walked toward my locker and ducked my head, running my tongue over my teeth to make sure nothing was caught in my elaborate braces situation. The eyes still followed. I patted my bangs, found them to be appropriately stiff with hairspray. What was the deal?

Then I noticed the locker signs.

Peppered among the gun-metal-gray doors were beautifully lettered signs proclaiming a new extracurricular: The KHK Club. I passed a few of the signs before getting close enough to see the asterisk at the bottom. The bubble letters were crisply lined in Sharpie:

*KHK = KIDS HATE KIM

Helga and her minion, Dummy McDummerson,* watched me from behind Helga's open locker door. I felt my eyes sting and I blinked furiously, turning my curved shoulders toward my own locker and busying myself with taking off my coat, hanging up my backpack, pretending that a club dedicated to hating me was no big deal. Just another Tuesday. Whatevs. Blink the tears and set the jaw. Bell's about to ring.

I don't remember anything about the rest of that day. Helga and I went to a Christian elementary school, so my guess is that some eagle-eyed teacher noticed the hate campaign and forced Helga to sit down for a devotional or something. The signs were probably gone by lunchtime. I remember seeing a couple of them crumpled on the floor, already stepped on and bearing sneaker tread markings. Maybe Helga apologized. Maybe she had to write a Bible verse about the wickedness of the tongue one hundred times on the chalkboard. I don't remember.

I do remember being pummeled with the sudden realization that I should never assume people understood what I was about. I'd thought that Helga, while inconsistent, was mostly my friend.

---

*   Not her real name.

Helga was not. Helga made hate literature about me during her extracurricular hours.

We won't always be understood by the people around us. And we get to decide if we take on pronouncements and descriptions and locker signs that try to force us into someone else's neat and tidy narrative or if we keep a really good eraser handy in case we come upon a decree that doesn't tell the truth. We get to decide if we let another person tell us to smut up, burn our book, keep quiet, get angry, pipe down. It works out best if we choose wisely. It works out best if we turn around before the bell rings and let the world see our real face again, even if it's streaked with tears. We get to decide who holds the Sharpie.

One hard-won hint: Helga isn't the girl for the job.

PEOPLE FALL FOR mistaken identities all the time. We really have to get better at sniffing this junk out. This reminds me of the Swedes.

I'm Dutch, so as an outgrowth of my ethnocentrism, hardly anything reminds me of the Swedes. But mistaken identities do.

One morning in 1981, some folks living on the coast of Sweden woke to a gigantic Soviet sub perched on their shore. It was alarming. This was the Cold War, and unless your name was Sean Connery, you were not going to get a parade when you showed up in a sub with the sickle and hammer on the side. After some hemming and hawing, the Swedes sent a few Welcome Wagon reps out to the boat, and they knocked on the door. When the Soviet sailors opened the hatch, they explained that their coordinates were off and they'd accidentally beached their super-secret sub in an inopportune location.

The Swedes nodded and then asked, "Can we take a look around?"

The Soviets said no. They could not.

The Swedes knew it had been a long shot, so they took it well and ended up helping to ease the sub back into international waters and waved it on its way.

When the sub was at a safe distance, Sweden wigged out. They realized that while being a neutral country had its perks, those perks felt pretty flimsy when a Soviet sub loomed in their port. So they took quick action and beefed up their navy. Top priority was now patrolling the waters around the thousands of miles of shoreline, and since even Swedish people can't be everywhere at once, they decided to use clues to track down enemy subs.

They dedicated millions of dollars and thousands of hours and hundreds of military personnel to this operation. The goal was to listen for the subs, and they started hearing solid evidence of their presence almost immediately. The sound became well known among sailors, and they even named it: Typical Sound. The subs were making this sound, and it started really ticking off the Swedes. The president of Sweden even wrote an angry letter to Gorbechev when the Cold War was supposed to be over and they were still picking up sub sounds. Gorbechev said he had no idea what the president was talking about and to just calm down already.

I have some embarrassing news: The Typical Sounds were not enemy subs lurking in deep waters. The Typical Sound was herring farts.

This is not the way you want to open a press conference, but I suppose someone had to break the news. Hundreds of people, millions of dollars, twelve years—all dedicated with the earnestness of your favorite Swedish uncle, and misdirected toward gassy fish.

We are so easily fooled, aren't we? We pick up a couple bits of feedback from those around us and decide that our identity is fixed. If someone said we weren't enough, we believe them. If our parents took their own hurt and unleashed it on us, we agree that we aren't worth much better. If a person we admire told us the biggest of lies, that God needed us to clean up our act before we headed in His direction, we set out working on the unworkable and taking every detour available so we don't have to face His disappointment.

The editor who wanted me to sex up my book was wrong. I didn't follow her advice and that book ended up landing at a great publishing house filled with people who understood what I was trying to do and helped me get that book to lots and lots of readers. I still do a little sassy jig and dedicate it to the smut-advocate editor every time I get a royalty check for that novel.

Helga was wrong. Not all kids hate Kim. It was mostly Helga and Dummy and a boy who had asked me out and I'd declined because he made me nervous with his intensity. We were in fourth grade, dude. Stop staring at me during Library.

The Swedes were wrong. The Soviets might have been up to some nefarious things but one of them was not stalking the Swedish coast. That noise was something altogether different and super funny to every junior high boy from the history of the world onward.

We get to decide. Substance or flatulence. Stand steadfast in the truth or content ourselves with the easy lie. Seek out the real-down-deep or settle for the knockoff. The brushstrokes of people who love you with ferocity or Sharpies in dangerous hands. If the God who made you says you are beloved and beautiful and worth crossing time and space and all sorts of brokenness for, I think we would be absolutely nuts not to believe Him. Other voices might chime in, but before we scooch over and make room for them in our hearts, I think it works better to narrow our eyes and sniff for Sharpie. Don't be fooled: Just because words are loud and just because they might look like they're in permanent ink, one good swipe from a strong hand can bring them tumbling down.

PART III

TRIED AND TESTED

I KNOW OF A MAN WHO MADE A POT OF MONEY BUT kept it all for himself. Folks in town knew he had done well for himself, well enough that maybe he'd spare some extra for a donation to the softball team or the firefighters' fund or the church. The man said no. He said it every time he was asked, and he wasn't particularly gentle about it. He came to be known as the guy who kept to himself, both with his presence and with his treasure.

When this man died a few years ago, he had stacks of actual gold lined up around his bed. He'd physically surrounded himself with his money, perhaps as a wall of defense, perhaps as a reminder to anyone who asked that he had worked hard, won much, gathered well.

The strangest part of this story is that after the man's death, the town heard what happened to all that treasure. The man gave it away, bestowing in his absence shockingly large sums to a few charities of his choice, all of which had asked for help during his lifetime and all of which he'd flatly refused. The man had riches upon riches, but he didn't put them to use while he still had a front-row seat. He didn't take that gold for a test run, try it out, see what it could do.

Grace is not an idea. Grace is not a theory. It's not something we hear about, nod in agreement, and then leave in stacks around our house. We don't keep grace in a petri dish and hypothesize about what might happen if we unleash it into the real world.

Grace is meant to be road tested. We're supposed to take it out for a spin the second after we first hear about it. There is no on-ramp. There is no preliminary course of study before we get to watch for grace, gather grace to ourselves, give grace away as if we'll have plenty more where that came from.

God loves action verbs when it comes to our experience with him and with his grace. Taste and see, he urges. Test me. Follow me. Watch me. I'll show you things that will knock your socks off. Trust me, you don't want to miss this, and you will miss it if you just agree with me but don't let this stuff loose in your life. Grace upon grace upon grace, and it's ours, right now and forever for the taking.

GRIEF

WHEN ANA WAS ABOUT A YEAR AND A HALF OLD, and the endless Midwestern winter finally broke and gave way to the Technicolor green of spring, we drove to my hometown for Easter. We were living out of state at the time so Marc could finish his millionth year of graduate school, and I was practically panting for a visit home. I knew my parents would do what they were becoming pros at doing, which was to devote themselves entirely to indulging their only grandchild. This, along with a series of days when I would not be the only one cooking, cleaning, diapering, and trying to shower by four in the afternoon, would mean a break for me.

Also, He is risen.

My parents had undergone wholesale personality shifts with the birth of their grandbaby. I felt like an anthropologist when I would study their absolutely foreign behavior. They forgot every form of discipline they'd used with me and my siblings. Take cereal, for example. If things got positively wild when I was growing up, my parents would allow us to eat Raisin Bran. They would look the other way with the sugar-sprinkled raisins. *Raisins* triggered celebration.

Upon her birth, Ana was given Froot Loops and Cocoa Puffs, whichever she preferred. And if eight cups a day weren't enough, my dad would fly to the grocery store, driving at irresponsible speeds, to buy more.

Up to this point, I was unclear if my dad knew where the grocery store was located.

And then there was safety. My dad was a reliable source of laughter-crying while my siblings and I grew up. I know you know this phenomenon. When someone is launching you in the air in the pool and you are laughing at the flip in your stomach and the height you are soaring and then also crying because you know you'll have to go all the way back down and that water can feel a lot harder than it looks? That's laughter-crying, and my dad was the master. Each summer, we would visit a go-kart track, and my dad's singular goal was to get kicked out for reckless driving. I rode with him in the passenger seat because, while laughter-crying was a given, it was better than looking over my shoulder and seeing him howling maniacally, ball cap on backward, and knowing he was about to crash into your cart and leave you spinning into a pile of stacked tires.

Better to make friends with the lunatic.

I have vivid recollections of my dad swinging my brother around in circles, Ryan hiccupping with laughter, hands gripping my dad's hands as they made their own human pinwheel on our front lawn, right before Ryan's hiccups turned to yowls when his shoulder popped out of its joint and Dad had to force it back in.

When his granddaughter arrived, Dad forgot entirely who he was. That person no longer existed. He was no longer Renegade. No longer Maverick. No longer Shoulder Popper.

He was now Safety Ranger.

If Marc toted around toddler Ana on his shoulders, my dad would purse his lips and ask if we were sure that was safe. He would then ignore our response and walk behind Marc as a spotter. When I mentioned the idea of a future sleepover at the home of Ana's little friend, Dad shot me a glance to kill and cited terrifying statistics involving elder siblings and role playing. Sleepovers were a thing of the past, he said. There was no reason to play with fire.* When Ana wandered near an electrical cord, outlet, or battery, my dad would blow by her, scooping up all those things and gathering all the lamps, cords, and electrical appliances in the house and crowding them on top of the dining room table, out of reach.

I would catch the eye of my mom, who might have shrugged in solidarity if she hadn't been busy layering Ana's high chair tray with Oreos and spray whipped cream.

Easter at home was a gift, and I was so, so ready to share that time with my parents. Dad grinned and my mom squealed when we pulled up, jogging to the back door of our car so they

---

* I went on no fewer than seven thousand sleepovers before the age of thirteen. Apparently I was really good with fire.

could extricate Ana from a seat crusty with Goldfish confetti. I hugged my mom, Marc hugged my dad, we all hugged each other. And we did the same ritual when, a little bit later, we told them we were pregnant again. We were having another baby. Let the indulgence continue!

My dad teared up. My mom danced with Ana and pressed her cheek to mine.

"I'm so happy for you," she said into my ear, mindful always of how long it had taken for us to get pregnant with Ana. She'd walked that hard and lonely road with me, and now that road seemed to be suddenly smooth, uncomplicated.

We had a great weekend. We saw everyone I'd ever known at church that Sunday, and we told every one of them that I was pregnant. It was a beautiful few days.

The first day back at our house in Nebraska, I lost the baby.

I was thirteen weeks along.

☆ ☆ ☆

I'VE DECIDED THAT the best way to comfort someone who is getting walloped by grief is to stop talking precisely one sentence before you would like to stop talking. Those last sentences are just unfailingly stupid. My guess is that they cross into stupid because last sentences try to summarize. Wrap things up. Push us on our way with a little lilt in our step.

Last sentences are American. Americans love lilt.

I know people are trying to help when they put pretty bows on suffering. I really think they assume they're making it better when they shift the conversation to a sunshiny tone. The trouble is, that approach just doesn't work. As my mom would say, "Bless their hearts for trying." As I would say, "Please stop talking, you insufferable person."

In no particular order of offense, here are a few last sentences to avoid when talking with someone who is mourning the loss of her baby:

- "God has a plan." Note: I am aware. And from my vantage point, His plan breaks my heart.
- "Everything happens for a reason." Note: Theologically sound. So is the original meaning behind animal sacrifice. Perhaps we could revisit both of those things on a day that my eyelids aren't swollen from weeping.
- "You're young. You can have more." I choose not to comment on this one because of Jesus and His request that I cuss less this year.
- "That baby must have had some serious health problems. Nature's way of taking care of it." I remember a low moan starting in my chest and throat when I endured these words. I wanted every version and every part and every story of the babies I lost. Nature didn't ask me my opinion.
- (Nodding to Ana, who was playing nearby:) "At least you've already had one baby, so you know your body knows how." My body knew nothing, as far as I could tell. My body had a long memory for being barren and a short memory for everything else. My bones ached with memory, and I didn't have anywhere to put that ache.

I blame us all for these failed attempts at comfort. I really love my country, but we just don't do mourning very well around here. We should do better. Like the Italians, who bake special cookies with almond and butter and cloves and cinnamon and pass them around to honor the ones they've lost. I imagine the house filling with the scent of spices and butter and sugar as the cookies bake, and I bet smelling that comfort cocktail could make a girl feel a little less lost for a moment.

Or we could be like the bereaved in Greece and Portugal and wear black to show an outward expression of inward emptiness. Forty days in black for the Greeks and a lifetime for Portuguese widows. Maybe a lifetime would seem a bit much, or maybe it would seem just right. But I bet it feels good to physically *do* something, put on something, tug on a sweater or a skirt or tie a hair ribbon in the perfect shade of how I feel. To let my appearance make sense to me and to the people around me.

Or we could sit shiva like Jewish mourners. We could open our homes for seven days after burying someone we love and just be together. Give each other the dedicated space and time to grieve. I could be romanticizing this. Maybe after Day 2, all you want is for people to get the heck out of your house and stop asking you if they can get you some more casserole or another cup of coffee. Then again, maybe that's the point. Maybe the daily-ness of being together helps a girl move into and out of the first sting of loss, enough so that on Day 8, when you're standing on your porch alone, you luxuriate in the silence and the chance to make your own lunch or no lunch at all.

I had none of these things when I lost my babies. There would be two. One that spring in Nebraska and another two years later. I didn't have a way to mark the passage of time and the waves of grief other than a calendar that marched mercilessly onward and a toddler who didn't see anything wrong with me crying while I scooped her a helping of mac and cheese.

A lot of people had a lot of things to say, but I wish some of them would have stopped before that last sentence. The last part didn't help and sometimes hurt. I really needed them *not* to know why this was happening. I really needed them to tell me they didn't have one earthly idea how to fix it, but that they knew it wasn't my fault that my body seemed broken.

I needed an almond cookie and a black cardigan. Those things would have helped.

THE MOST COMFORTING thing I've ever heard about grief has to do with animals. It's not a fuzzy and cute image of animals, so don't get your hopes up. It has to do with snorting.

I think it was Tim Keller, a pastor in Manhattan, where there are no livestock but there are smart theologians, who gave this and many other gifts to my spirit and mind with his teaching over the years. He was telling the story of Lazarus, the guy best known for being raised from the dead. Jesus did the raising, and it's even more beautiful than a general raising-from-dead story* because Lazarus was one of Jesus' best friends. This wasn't a death Jesus read about in the paper. This death was personal.

So when Jesus approached the tomb of His friend, and He saw all the other people who loved Lazarus the way He did, and He heard their crying and saw the dark circles under their eyes

---

* Not sure there are any "general" ones, but stay with me.

and the blotchy spots on their cheeks, He bellowed. The word in Greek says Jesus snorted like an animal. He wept and He cried and He raged and He bellowed like an animal in *anger*. That's the part that gets me. Jesus, of all people, knew a lot about what was waiting for Lazarus and that death was not permanent. And yet Jesus was furious. He was angry at death and all the ways it robs us and hurts us and takes from us. He was angry because He knew more than anyone that we aren't built for death. Our spirits don't know how to do it because they weren't made for it.

They were made for forever.

When I got back from the hospital, limping and worn out, emptied of my little one and in every possible way, I sat next to Marc on the couch. My mind ran laps, trying to land on something firm, some steady ground to explain loss. I'd done all the right things, I'd thought. I'd relied on my tried-and-true, the reading, the planning, the avoiding of deli meat and alcohol and the embracing of folic acid and Mozart CDs and plenty of sleep. I'd worked my way, but my work hadn't been enough. My neat and tidy hadn't been enough.

I clutched Marc's hand and willed its warmth into me. I'd been so cold in the recovery room, I couldn't stop shaking. I remember a nurse seeming a little miffed that I needed another blanket, and then another, and another, and nothing could really warm me up and stop my arms and legs from trembling.

Marc held my hand and I wept. I bellowed. None of this was fair. I didn't want it.

I looked over at my husband. Tears streamed down his face, the face I loved so much and wanted to watch for all our days together. Marc is always stronger than I am, and I needed an infusion of that strength.

He drew in a shaky breath, and with tears falling down his cheeks, he said, "'The Lord gives.'" Tears fell off the edge of his jaw. "'And the Lord takes away.'" He swallowed hard. "I'm going to bless His name anyway."

I still don't know how Marc had the courage to say those words that day. This was the same man who had once argued with me that humans should live a life without suffering because that approach would make everything more efficient. God could just tell us stuff, he'd said, and we would listen and write it down and grow and skip the suffering bit.

We've walked through plenty of loss since then, though, and I know those words cost him but he said them anyway. He believed them anyway. He let me hold his strong hand while he believed and I bellowed, and together, the math added up to enough for that day and the day after that.

Maybe one of the most ferocious things about grace is that it pushes into the most dangerous, most precarious moments and holds us tight. It doesn't crowd out the untidiness but it's not intimidated by it either. And grace most certainly does not ask us to hurry up our broken hearts. I had no capacity to strive for one single thing during the days my heart was wiped out by grief. There were no A's to earn in this class. There were only hours to face. There were only questions followed immediately by unsatisfactory answers. The grace of God in those days looked like warm blankets resting on shaky limbs. It looked like a warm hand that wouldn't leave mine, even as I careened from one unsteady moment to the next.

And that same grace didn't falter when I didn't muster the strength to pray like a good girl. I'd been real busy trying to say the right things to God, do the right things with my prenatal body, pray the right prayers to get what I wanted, which was an easy pregnancy, a healthy baby, and a neat avoidance of suffering. Those days, though, taught me a little about what God really thinks about my nice girl speeches. He's not as into them as I'd thought. In fact, I think it saddens God a bit when we try to wrap up shattered pieces into pretty containers with gaudy satin bows. I think He prefers some bellowing because the bellowing is honest. I think He's okay with us dropping off, midthought, and not finishing the last sentence. We are fragile, and He knows it. We are courageous, too, and He knows it, long before we know it ourselves.

We were made for forever. Most days, it feels like the bravest act in the world to tuck that hope, that tenacious promise of grace, in our trembling hands and just keep walking, holding fast to it and making our way along rough, uneven road.

ROUGH SEAS

USED TO BE A HIGH SCHOOL SPANISH TEACHER.
What are you envisioning right now? Here are some options:

1. Quirky woman with a bad perm, chanting the days of the week *en español.*
2. Quirky, permed woman wearing a black, sequined sombrero in the middle of a workday.
3. Quirk-Perm walking too quickly through a crowded school hallway, a stack of papers in her arms that doesn't quite cover her embroidered blouse she bought on her last trip to Bolivia, all of which she mentions to you as she scurries, ending with an exaggerated pronunciation of the word "Boh-lee-vee-ah."

4. Quirkita refusing to "understand" her students when they speak to her *en inglés*. ESPAÑOL, PEPITO, POR FAVOR.

5. Q using an abundance of upside-down exclamation points in all written correspondence, never mind that the document is in English. *¡Watch those verb endings, Charo!*

Everything you are picturing is true. Spanish teachers are a breed.

There are exceptions, of course, and by that I mean everyone I personally know or have worked with or was mentored by. I don't want to burn any bridges.* But all the other Spanish teachers are wackadoodle.

I've been to a lot of continuing education with this crew. I don't want to revisit how many times I've heard "La Bamba" sung by rooms full of foreign language educators who have mistaken a conference room for a pub. No sangria in sight, and yet "*¡Yo no soy marinero!*" ricocheted off the folding chairs, orthopedic clogs a-swaying to the beat.

One of my first teaching jobs was at a high school in a small town in eastern Iowa. My commute was fifty minutes each way on a two-lane highway, unless either I got stuck by fog, which often moved in waves across the rolling hills that lined the road, or I got behind a tractor. Tractors do not speed. Under any circumstance. And they don't pull over onto teeny tiny gravel shoulders so that a Spanish teacher can get to work on time. She should

---

* Writing is a completely impractical career choice. I could be back in the classroom wielding my maracas by the time you reach the end of this sentence.

have been a math teacher anyway. Give those kids some skills so we can compete with China!

When I signed on to that job, I was young and young and young, and I looked like it. When I would later substitute-teach in Iowa City while earning my graduate degree, I would regularly get stopped by other teachers, and they would demand a hall pass. It was awkward for both of us when I explained I was teaching there for the day. For money. And had been filing my own taxes for years.

The same thing happened in the halls of the school where I taught after that long commute. The day before classes started in the fall, I was walking toward my new classroom, a window-less room with cinder block walls painted in slick yellow paint, and I heard a slow wolf whistle from a few paces behind me. I turned to see who I would later know as Lonny Nichols. Lonny walked with a strut, and he lifted his chin in greeting when I turned around.

"Hey," he said, a slow smile working its way across his braces.

"Hey," I returned, lifting my own chin. "I'm the new Spanish teacher."

Lonny's half smile froze at that bit of news.

I turned around and called, "¡Hasta mañana!"

It was a rough semester for Lonny, as I recall.

One of my assignments during that year, in addition to chaperoning prom, for which I was paid fifty American dollars,* was

---

* This was not enough compensation, because I am still scarred by having to run over to the DJ during the last song and strongly suggest that he change it from "I'll Make Love to You" to something a little less OBVIOUSLY STUPID AS A WAY TO SEND HUNDREDS OF TEENAGERS OUT INTO THE NIGHT OF THEIR SENIOR PROM.

to take a group of students to Spain. Nine high school girls, most of whom had never been out of the country and some who hadn't been out of the state. I absolutely adored those girls. Traveling with them was, as we say in the Great Midwest, a hoot.

About halfway into our travels, we took a day trip to Morocco, and on the way back to Spain, while crossing the Strait of Gibraltar, we nearly perished.

I realize we haven't known each other long, and I know you might think that because I've written some novels, I tend to dramatize moments. Maybe you've pegged me as an exaggerator. I want to assure you there is not one bit of hyperbole here: *We almost died.* Every last one of us, not to mention a ferry full of additional day-trippers. Dead. It was nearly the Ferry of Death.

You know in those Bible stories when storms just descend out of nowhere and people wig out and start crying? Like the sailors on Jonah's rogue ship headed to Tarshish instead of Nineveh? Or pretty much every time the disciples head out on the water with Jesus and become highly annoyed because Jesus is sleeping and not attending to their panic? I used to judge those people severely. What a bunch of pansies, I would think. I live in Iowa. We have big, beautiful, endless sky, and so we tend to have a lot of warning when a storm is about to hit. There are signs, so you need to pay attention, but there's no reason to lose your mind over it.

Travel expands our horizons. In this instance, my horizon expanded to the spot juuuust next to maritime death.

A hot, sunny day turned on a dime as we were cruising at a clip over the blue waters of the Strait, and within minutes, waves crashed with wild abandon over the decks of the ship. The long, flat cabin where we were sitting in rows became gradually quiet as we watched the sea swell just outside the walls of windows. The room tilted and the ship started to groan. I watched my girls, their eyes growing wider with the second. Panic was starting to settle in among the other passengers. I remember with great clarity a Spanish teacher from another school crawling (you read that correctly: crawling) on her hands and knees up the aisle, her wide-brimmed sun hat sitting diagonally askew on her hair. I also remember the man who sat in front of me gripping the metal pole near his chair with two beefy hands, holding on to it while he moaned and sweated through his shirt.

For my part, I kept things light! Told some jokes! Used my exclamation points freely! The girls stared at me, then they would glance at the aisle crawler, then look back at me with questions on their faces. Was now the time to freak out? they said with their faces. Because it felt like a very organic time to freak out.

I remember praying out loud. Technically, I was a public school teacher, but technically, we were about to croak. Prayer was allowed. I remember praying, I remember the sweaty pale guy, and I remember my girls being remarkably calm, taking the time to comfort each other when fear took hold.

I was so young and dumb. What on earth were these parents thinking, letting me take their daughters halfway around the world? I was about forty seconds out of puberty myself. I had no business leading anyone anywhere.

I knew nothing. I made jokes and tried to distract and kept an eye on which girl was going to vomit. I knew nothing, and yet God calmed the storm. We weathered it, He calmed it.

I knew nothing, but I did know I had absolutely no ability to calm a Mediterranean squall. My paycheck did not cover that skill set.* I was able to sit and weather and pray and try to lift our thoughts out of total despair. But the storm was God's to tackle.

We really don't do ourselves any good when we try to change the weather. It's remarkable how often I forget this, and I'm guessing you might have the same problem. When I'm in the midst of heartache or loss or pain, I can get very busy, very fast, trying to stop the squall. How can I best hurry through this moment and get to another one I like better? What can I try to control or tamp down in order to skip this part? How can I boss around someone or let them know how I think they should act in order to fix this day, this conversation, this relationship? Let me at it, I seem to say to anyone who will listen. This is a horrible storm and I'm sick of the waves and my stomach is roiling and I am going to *will* it to be over.

Just like on that wind-walloped day on the ferry, when I let messy, frantic prayers pour out of my heart and into the storm, surrendering does help, if I let it. And if I mean it. When all seems lost and I have absolutely nothing left, my prayers are the most honest. I bring nothing to the table in those moments, so there's no other way to talk to God. Even I know that tossing my orange life jacket up into the howling wind will not convince the skies to clear. So honest prayer it is. Letting strivings cease it is. Telling God I am in desperate need of His grace it is. The life jacket, any shiny thing I can offer to God, that's all pretty useless.

---

* It also didn't cover, say, a new pair of jeans. Teachers are the working poor, and don't you ever forget it and don't you dare let one holiday go by without buying them really nice stuff.

✩ ✩ ✩

GOD HEARD US, and that storm died down as quickly as it had sprung up. We disembarked onto Spanish soil where the sun was already reclaiming its dominance. Sweaty guy shakily picked up right where he'd left off and went to nab a plate of paella.

There's this beautiful little line in the Jonah story where the guy who ran away has come back and is talking honestly to God for once. I can identify. Sometimes it takes a few wind-sprints for me to start saying what's true. Jonah is in this honest space, and he notices that "those who cling to worthless idols forfeit the grace that could be theirs." The grace that's mine is fully available to me. The grace that has your name written beautifully all over it? It's yours for the taking, even in the middle of the wind and waves. We can get in the way, though. We can forfeit it all and make the passage through the storm infinitely more treacherous for ourselves.

What are our fingers grasping, white-knuckled with slippery grip, even though we know what we are holding won't save, redeem, or rescue? Our pride? Our anger? Our hurt? Our need to control circumstances or the people around us? Our carefully laid plans that refuse to cooperate? What worthless thing are we clinging to that's getting in the way of the grace that is ours?

When I read about Jesus walking on the water and silencing storms with a word, I breathe more deeply now. I don't judge the pansies as harshly.* They were totally out of control in those moments, and we are too. They were not and we are not at all equipped to quiet a storm. We are not the fixers. We

---

* Except for Judas.

are the weatherers. We call out our clumsy, honest prayers, we crack ill-timed jokes, we hold on to each other, and we watch the waves. And we wait on the One who calms sudden squalls with one word. He is not far off when we reach for Him, frantic, tired, wondering how, exactly, we got to be where we are. Grace that lifts up and smooths out is not beyond the scope of the storm. Meeting us in the spots where we are fully overwhelmed and underqualified is not one step outside of God's pay grade and skill set.

Eyes on Him, arms around each other, we wait for His command for the wind and waves to obey. They do. They're no match for Him. In fact, they don't stand a chance.

BETTER NOT
TO KNOW

ONE REALLY GOOD REASON GOD DOESN'T SUBMIT His agenda to me is that I would constantly be calling meetings. My concerns erupt on an hourly basis some days.

Are you sure, God, that this is the best course of action?

Should we revisit this plan? Let's take a look at what You have in mind so I can correct it. You know how I love a new red pen! Time to put that thing to *work*!

Are you sure You want this for me? There are about eight hundred other options we should strongly consider.

I am full of suggestions, and I give them freely, even though my eyesight compromises my view.

☆ ☆ ☆

MARC AND I got married in a blizzard. Blizzards happen in the Midwest, and usually this means we hunker down in our homes, make chili and cinnamon rolls, and watch a movie featuring Colin Firth. Or at least that's what we do at our house. But when you're pretty much committed to getting married that day, you have to put on the dress and tux and the chili has to wait.

Iowans are hearty, so a little snow and ice don't impress. This storm, however, immobilized. Two interstates closed. They *closed*, as in orange-barrel barricades across exits, no entry, no exit. No cars were allowed to be on them, not even ambulances or Amazon Prime. I can't remember another time this happened, but trust me that a lot of people couldn't get to the wedding.* Our families did, though, and many friends, our wedding party, and my uncle, who is the pastor who married us. It all worked out. We got hitched.

And stayed hitched, even though I know we both had second thoughts. Marc's first doubts must have creeped in when we called my parents' house the next morning to let them know we'd be bringing by my wedding gown before we flew out for

---

* Reverential shout-out here to my feisty college roommate, Alyssa, who is the most determined person I know. She made it from Chicago. Drove through drifts and maybe a couple humans to get to us. Her passage defied logic. I will never forget turning to look down the aisle during our rehearsal and seeing her standing in the foyer of the church, wild mane of red hair backlit, standing arms crossed and wearing moon boots. The woman is a legend. She now teaches in the Chicago Public Schools, earned her doctorate while skiing moguls of a pandemic, corrals her diverse neighborhood into a thriving community, and organizes earth. We saw all of this coming.

some dental school interviews in California.* My dad picked up the phone.

"It's the happy couple!" he crowed into the receiver. I could hear a house full of relatives brunching in the background. And then he asked, "Is it official? Is the marriage consummated?"

I rolled my eyes. "Dad, that is—"

"It's official!" he shouted to the room. "The marriage is consummated!"

I heard a lot of laughter and a cheer, probably from my grandma.

Marc, who was listening, looked a lot like a person who wanted to be invisible forever.

In my defense, or in defense of my insane family, Marc wasn't the only one entitled to second thoughts. About a month later, after wrapping up the interview tour, shipping off a pile of wedding thank-you notes, and moving to Costa Rica, Marc and I took a short honeymoon. This was before Google, so when I consider how we pulled it all off, I have more respect for how intrepid it was. We packed a small bag, strapped on our Chacos, and struck out to the western coast and its pristine beaches.

One afternoon during that trip, as the sun started to dip lazily into the ocean, Marc and I sat in the sugar-fine sand, alternatively staring at the water and then at each other. I was overcome with gratitude. First, that we hadn't died in the school bus Marc had made us take at 2 that morning because he was too frugal to pay for an actual bus. The bus driver was a man actively drinking hard liquor while a nubile girl one-fourth his age draped herself

---

*   Romance = Dental school!

around his shoulders. We were all able to watch this interaction in the oversized visor mirror that hung above the driver's seat. It was harrowing.

Our survival of the Nubile Bus Ride was the first reason I was feeling grateful. And second, despite his issues with spending money on safe travel practices, I was gobsmacked with gratitude for Marc. He was really great, and I'd married him. I'd won the freaking relationship lottery! I started to tell him.

"Babe," I said, my face close to his, eyes locked on his, "I love you. More than yesterday. I'm so grateful for you and for this adventure and all the ones waiting for us, and I'm so glad you chose *me*."

I thought the speech was pretty good. Turquoise water, sun setting, me, young and scantily clad, close enough to kiss. All in all, I gave myself high marks.

Marc narrowed his eyes and here is his response, verbatim:

"When I'm this close to you, you look like a cyclops."

Listen, I was in it for the long haul. I didn't decide this was my cue to make an exit stage left.

I'm just saying it's natural to wonder if you've made the right choice.

☆ ☆ ☆

THE THING IS, we just don't know a lot. We think we do, but we aren't reliable judges. Take, for example, Galileo. Boy, did we call that one wrong. The guy had some serious guts, asserting that everyone else was mistaken and that we weren't, in fact, the center of the universe. Turns out, we agree now that he was right.* Before we got to that, though, we excommunicated Galileo for his brilliance and for his unwillingness to pipe down. How embarrassing!

And those medieval people weren't the only ones to get it wrong when it comes to space and our place in it. Remember Pluto? Every mobile you made in elementary school is a pile of hooey. That song about pizza** is total bunk.

I'm saying that we do the best with what we know and that since we know so little, we need to be ready-handed with grace.

God sure is. When He talks about the way He loves us, He says it's lavish. Extravagant. Wide and deep like the ocean. Expansive like the stars.

I understand this a little more after having kids. I love them in a way that does not reflect their behavior. I don't wait for them to understand the workings of the universe before I give them a bear hug or bake their favorite cookie or give them a winter coat that can make it through a blizzard. My kids get all of those things because they are my kids. They can be snotty and difficult. They can be fickle in their affections and clueless in their approaches to relationships. They can make me say things like, "You're all trying to kill me with your attitude issues," and "Perhaps you have forgotten that I birthed you after eight hours of hard labor without an epidural."

None of those rough days gets any traction, though, because these kids are mine. My love for them looks a lot less like a bunch

---

* Well, *some* of us do. There are some TikTokers who still take issue. TikTokers! Such low-hanging fruit!
** My Very Educated Mother Just Served Us Nine Pizzas. (Turns out your mom was wrong. There are eight pizzas.)

of orange barricades keeping people off the road and a lot more like the deep blue of an ocean teeming with life and stories and history.

God's love for you and me doesn't rest on what we can puzzle out about where the future is heading. He doesn't reserve His best grace for people who make the best plan. In fact, I find He tends to politely ignore my plans. Plans will kill an adventure every day of the week, and God's invitation to a life with Him will always lead with adventure. You can bring your pocket planner if you want, but I doubt you'll crack open that thing once.

I GET TO travel a bit for work, and I know that when I leave our zip code, I'd better have a Word doc on the kitchen counter. The Word doc is for one particular person. Ana is in college, so she is happily busy figuring out her own hours and minutes. Mitch doesn't typically realize I'm gone until it's a national holiday that involves baking. And Marc doesn't need written instructions because he can just ask Thea.

Thea loves detailed lists and agendas and Word docs detailing how everyone will navigate the hours ahead. She came out of the womb like this and has never deviated from her love of order. For example, when she returned home after trick-or-treating as a three-year-old ladybug, she spread out her haul on the kitchen floor and organized the candy into piles according to brand and color. She didn't eat one piece until everything was in order. Mitch and Ana watched like she was a zoo animal, their own cheeks stuffed with Snickers and Airheads.

If I start sentences with "Listen, when I die, someone will need to know this," I am only ever talking with Thea.

So Thea really surprised me one day on a Florida beach. This stretch of sand was thousands of miles from the one in Costa Rica when I first started learning that life was going to be disobedient to all my best-laid plans. Thea the planner taught me that clinging to the plan can make a girl miss out.

The day before, we'd visited that same beach. You would have known us by our alarmingly white skin. Midwesterners on spring break can really frighten people if they aren't ready to see every vein through translucent skin (Day 1) or the purple bruises a sunburn can achieve (Days 2 and following). On our first outing, Thea had been stung badly by a jellyfish, multiple times, right at the end of a day swimming and diving and body surfing her way to shore. She's a tough kid, but those stings put her out of commission for hours afterward. We had several days to go on our vacation, so I figured she'd take it easy when we tried the ocean again. My eyebrows shot up into my hairline, then, when we got to the beach on Day 2 and she started slathering sunscreen on before running back into the waves.

"You sure about this?" I narrowed my eyes at her over my sunglasses. "What about the jellyfish?"

And Thea, Ms. Word Doc herself, shrugged. "I've been thinking about that and here's the thing: Even if I'd known yesterday that I would be stung, I'd get in the ocean all over again because, Mom. Yesterday?" She paused, white dots of sunscreen freckling her face. "That was the *best* day."

Hard, beautiful, light- and dark-filled "yesterday" is the one we are living right now. We aren't always very good at recognizing it, but the truth is that even the yesterday that stings and drives us mad with the sudden change from joy to pain, even the day that hurts so much, even the day that takes us out of commission for a bit, that's the day that will end up showing the wave-wrestling was worth all the rough waters. If we just stay on the beach, protected under an umbrella and SPF 50, watching everyone else run into the surf but staying out of the fray ourselves, there's a good chance that our risk-free, daily planner perch will cost us. Thea reminds me that every day is a good opportunity to maybe glance at the Word doc plan and then leave that thing on the beach and enter the sapphire waters, rocky though they may be.

We aren't supposed to know the end of the story. We aren't really even that good at predicting the end of the sentence. When we remember God's ocean-love and boundless grace, when we really believe that those things are just the way He is and will always be, then we don't need to submit our agendas and our bullet points. We can just peel off our winter layers, turn our faces to the sun, and run, knowing that eventually, even if it's a day decades from now and one spent on the other side of Glory, we'll see our roughest days as way points to The Best Days. We'll reach the moment when we can finally see the full, expansive view, horizon to horizon, and on that day we'll end up saying, "I'd do it all again because all those yesterdays? The long hours that coupled joy and tears? Laughter and stings? Those yesterdays put stone after stone along the road to this day. So even the yesterdays were the best days because the yesterdays lit my path Home."

HUMILITY

WHEN WE KEEP OUR TOES FULLY BURIED IN THE dark, rich soil of grace, we are much better able to remember we are not that great. DO NOT WRITE ME ANGRY LETTERS. SIMMER DOWN A SEC SO WE CAN TALK ABOUT THIS.

I realize this is not going to garner me a lot of points in the era of world-domination-by-supreme-effort-and-unceasing-cheerleading-of-self, but we have our limits, you and I. They are fairly strict limits. For example, I cannot run the world. I also cannot run my own life. Or yours. I can't work hard enough, jump high enough, strive far enough, sleep little enough to be the person Instagram tells me is juuuuust out of reach.

I'm just not that great. Greatness does not belong to the average person. And we are all, ahem, very, delightfully, stubbornly average.

And that's just the achievement angle. Let's also address the moral angle. We are decidedly not great in that area too. Raise your hand if you've lived a sin-free day. Okay, afternoon. Okay, a sin-free *hour*. Put that hand down because you just blew it with the sins of pride and general cluelessness.

I'm not trying to ruin your day, but I feel like it's okay to be honest about this stuff. We are a people in want. We do not have our stuff together, and we are thirsty for some help, already. If we ever thought we had it all nipped and tucked, all our deficiencies and waywardness and destructive tendencies and idolatry-of-self taken care of, when we fell in love or bore a child or got a puppy, we were then forced to admit we are selfish and cranky and impossibly fixated on our own navels most of the time, amen.

We are created in the breathtaking image of God. We reflect the One who draped necklace after necklace of stars across endless obsidian sky. The life in our cells comes directly from the God who is deliberate in the way He creates and sustains and moves among and in us. Your smattering of freckles across your nose, the way your eyes shine when you laugh, your ability to win the 50-yard dash or do donuts in your wheelchair or curl your tongue into the shape of a half pipe—all these beauties are the mark of intention. God doesn't roll dice and He doesn't create "in general." You bear His signature. You are the product of intricate design, draft tables filled with detailed drawings, careful, sure hands moving with certainty on the potter's wheel.

All these things are true.

What absolutely remarkable creatures we are.

We are also petty and hungry and mean. We criticize and slam. We injure and deflect blame. We betray and lie and scissor-kick the hearts of people we're supposed to love. We obsess over our bodies and we punish our bodies. We pretend, dodge, and tear down our homes with our own hands.

All these things are true.

What absolutely remarkable creatures we are.

MY FRIEND LOUIE owns a start-up company. This means he will work a million hours a week for about ten years and then sell the company and take a really long nap and a trip to Turks and Caicos. And then he'll do it all over again because he'll forget how horrible it was. Start-ups are a lot like having babies.

Louie has to attend lots of meetings with fantastically wealthy people so that he can explain to them why they shouldn't, say, build that mini-chalet encrusted with diamonds for their Chinese Crested puppy named Jean-Paul and instead should invest in Louie's company. Louie is very warm and engaging, and he has the ability to make everyone feel really welcome and loved, so these meetings usually end well, with Louie tucking a check into his bag and the investor giving extra organic jerky to Jean-Paul.

One meeting, though, hit a few bumps. Louie was in town to pitch to a Very Well-Known Company. The figurehead of this company, it turned out, was in the building that day. A suddenly nervous man with a headset approached Louie and cleared his throat.

"He's here," the nervous man said. "He's in the building."

Louie is smart, so he intuited that "he" didn't mean Jesus, though in other situations that would have been an appropriate interpretation of the man's excitement. "Sounds good," Louie said as he watched the man's eyes dart to all the doors in the room.

"We have rules," the man continued, breathless, eye-darty. "Under no circumstances will you take a photo of Him."

Louie brandished his phone, hands up as if preparing for his Miranda Rights, and he slowly tucked the phone into his suit pocket.

"You will not speak to Him." The man swallowed hard. "Unless He, for some reason, speaks to you first. Be careful."

Louie nodded. He was worried for the nervous man, who had begun to mop rivulets of sweat that trickled down his forehead.

"And no eye contact." The man said these words slowly.

The wizard made his way through the building, his presence tracked by his minions. Louie knew that before the wizard's net worth had skyrocketed to the top handful of earners in the world, the wizard had once been a minion himself. No one else seemed to remember the wizard's origin story, though, and so the scramble became to accommodate all requests to cradle and protect the wizard's ego. What mattered now was that the wizard had become famous and now lived within the understanding that he no longer needed to actually see the people around him.

Louie is an emotionally healthy person, so he recognized this for the insanity that it was. He obeyed and didn't make eye contact with the wizard behind the curtain, but he also didn't leave with a check. The wizard had a photo shoot and a spin class, and so even though he was the one who had initiated the meeting, it turned out he was abruptly unavailable.

Louie left the building, but it sounds like humility had already made its exit long ago. All that was left was a pile of money and a lot of sweaty headsets.

WE AREN'T GREAT with humility. We live in a culture that trades in the currencies of résumés, ladder climbs, and upmanship. We like promotions. We like winning. We like thanking people while holding plaques and trophies. We like hierarchies, and we really like when we are in the section that gets to sing "We Are the Champions" on repeat.

When I read in the Bible about sackcloth and ashes, I have cultural whiplash. I don't own a single scrap of sackcloth. I prefer soft knits and joggers. I don't spend a lot of time prostrating myself on the ground, other than when I'm at yoga and they make me.

This isn't to say that humility is a foreign concept where I live. I live in the Midwest, and we take pretend-humility very seriously. We are master deflectors, for example. If you compliment me on my shoes, I am obliged to tell you where I got them on sale, that I'm not really sure if I even like them, and that I should really just give them to you because you'd be so much cuter in them. If you compliment me on my child's solo in the school musical, I am required to tell you how your own son, though absolutely tone-deaf and perpetually flummoxed by rhythm, shone onstage.

We are very practiced at deflecting, which seems kind of humble until a few of the onion layers peel off and you see that the root of deflecting is still self-preoccupation. It's still navel gazing. Faux humility wears a smile better, but it's a kissing cousin to pride. Whether I think of myself as untouchable, someone who can't abide the unsolicited eye contact of the underlings, or whether I think of myself as less than my worth and keep eyes to the ground, both of those ways of moving through the world are jacked up. They both miss the mark, and they are both rooted in a fixation of self.

So we have a big fat problem because this means we and God are on opposite teams. This is an issue. There's this really chilling verse in the Bible that says God actively opposes the proud. He plants himself in front of those who think too highly of themselves, and He opposes them. In the original Greek, that word "oppose" means to strap on weapons and line up to fight a battle. That verse makes the hair stand up on my neck. I'd really prefer that God fight for me, not against me.

And He does. He will. In fact, in another section of that same Bible, God says He longs to be gracious to us. This is not a passive stance. God doesn't just hope you'll swing by and pick up some grace. He *longs* to give us grace. He opposes our yahoo tendencies to get the best seat, garner the most applause, win at everything, every day. He knows that kind of life is the emptiest way to live. Instead, He offers something far more compelling: grace. And guess what kind of people get this lavishing of grace?

The humble kind.

☆ ☆ ☆

ONE WAY TO practice your humility muscle is to write a book and then let other people read it. This experience is a lot like gathering all the people who attended high school with you, offering them a chair and a cool drink, and telling them to watch you as you perform a Spice Girls tap-dancing-slash-hip-hop montage. Naked.

The night before my first book released, I called my friend Ginger and asked her if heart palpitations were normal. I hadn't considered myself an anxious person, but this book thing was unveiling some hitherto unexplored parts of my personality. Ginger assured me I was right on track. She had many published books and hyperventilating into a bag was just part of her prerelease ritual.

I'm sure authors of yore felt nervous to get their words out into the world, but online reviews have shifted the immediacy of opinion sharing into overdrive. When I first started writing (the era of yore), readers had to work fairly hard to let their voices be heard. If folks didn't like my books, they had to write an email and sometimes even letters on paper with envelopes and stamps. They had to contact the publisher directly. No one knew how to find me. I was busy slinging chicken nuggets and changing an obscene number of diapers at that stage, so this worked out well for everyone.

Now, however, Brenda from Bemidji can offer her thoughts on my book while she waits in line for her oil change. Two stars out of five, on the Interweb forever, long past when she even remembers my book and long past when she has traded her Camry for a Traverse.

Authors aren't alone here. Sure, writers and creatives are particularly touchy and the least fun people at parties. We know this.* However, we aren't the only ones having to row through these choppy waters. We are all at the mercy of near-constant feedback. The world is loud, and its most insistent playbook encourages us to think about ourselves all the time. We can obey that call, but I've never found any satisfaction in that lane. In fact, I usually end up running really fast and hard after something shimmery that turns out to be a mirage.

When I look at myself in the way I'm meant to look at myself, I see breath-catching stuff. I see a girl beloved. I see a girl who has exactly what she needs because the One who loves her knows her better than she knows herself. I see a girl who has a ways to go in terms of character growth and wisdom and unselfishness and remembering what truly matters. But that same girl is fully equipped to tackle this next stretch of road, not because of any inflated or deflated self-publicity but because she's learning to walk lockstep with the God who will take her to all the best places.

Hers is the God who loves healthy humility. The God who doesn't avoid eye contact. The God who longs to give her grace.

C. S. Lewis wrote about humility as a great relief, an escape from "all the silly nonsense about your own dignity which has made you restless and unhappy all your life."** Goodness, doesn't that just make you want to lay down the silliness? To take off, as Lewis says, the "ugly, fancy-dress in which we have all got ourselves up and are strutting about like the little idiots we are." C. S. Lewis may call us little idiots because (a) he's British and (b)

---

* James Joyce, for example, wallpapered his house with his rejection slips. Feels a bit much.

** Lewis, C. S. *Mere Christianity*. San Francisco: Harper One, 2023.

we know he's right. Playing dress-up is no substitute for real dignity, real rescue, the real self-image we find when we see ourselves as sons and daughters of the One True King.

I have a suspicion that the more we see ourselves in the light that spools out like ribbons from God and onto our upturned faces, the more we find that humility is the true upgrade. We are remarkable creatures, made by hand. We don't need the posing and the posturing and the yapping and the chest bumps.

We need only to keep asking God what He thinks of us.

His answer will be, in the words of Lewis, like a drink of cold water to a man in a desert. His answer will take our breath away.

MATRIARCH

MY MATERNAL GRANDMA LIVED THE MAJORITY OF her years within seven miles of the spot where she was born. Her name was Edna Mae, and she was feisty. I suspect I take after her.

Grandma lived a full and exuberant life. She was not very easily dissuaded from either fullness or exuberance, hard times and happy times included. Grandma's family farm was leveled by a tornado when she was nineteen. The funnel destroyed her home, her family's crops, and their livestock. It scooped up my grandpa's love letters and spiraled them upward and outward for miles. Months later, as they were breaking up ground for spring planting, folks on faraway farms found letters strewn in their fields and mailed them to the address on the envelopes. This always struck me as a kindness, but Grandma was irked that those turkeys had clearly read the letters before sending them back to her. Voyeurs, she said with an eye roll.

Edna married my grandpa, Leon, during the Second World War. She wore a simple white jacket and matching skirt, and she held a white Bible with a little bouquet of lilies of the valley perched on its cover. My grandpa wore his Navy dress whites. They posed for their wedding portrait in front of an American flag. They were married for fifty-nine years. I have easy and free memories of them dancing in the kitchen and laughing like teenagers. My grandpa loved to brag that Grandma was voted Best Legs in college.* She would laugh when he'd tell that story, which, of course, made him want to tell it again.

A few of Edna's jobs: English and drama teacher, jewelry saleswoman, shop owner, mother of four, inspirational speaker, Bible teacher, Easter pageant director. She was one of the only women in her town in northwest Iowa who employed a babysitter. She needed childcare so she could work as a teacher, yes, for the income, but also so she could feed a part of her brain that she loved. She did this in the 1950s. She was a fire starter.

I've been thinking about Grandma a lot lately. She had four children over the course of nineteen years, stats that seem impossibly large to me since I am white-knuckling it with three offspring of my own. Maybe it's because I was her granddaughter and had the indulgence of not being the one she told to fold laundry or take out the trash, but my grandma always seemed unflappable to me. She seemed sure. Put together. Unconcerned about the future because she'd found her mettle

---

* I am not the recipient of this genetic gift. I have man calves. Please see "Stay in Your Lane," below, for a more thorough discussion.

during a Great Depression and a war, so how worried, really, did we need to be about anything when it came down to it?

I, on the other hand, am fully flappable. I get whipped up about things that do not deserve the thought time I devote to them. Here are some examples, every one of them an actual occurrence on the day of this writing:

1. Shoes piled by the back door really irritate me. There is a closet with a shoe rack DIRECTLY IN FRONT OF THE PILE, but that is too far for some. I have been known to holler like a stuck pig about shoes by the back door. I get wild-eyed and scary. My children have thrown around the word "demon" to describe my reactions. About *shoes*.

2. Some members of our household open every cabinet and cupboard and leave them in the yawning, exposed positions. Same with the dishwasher. And closet doors. And THE GAPING WOUNDS OF MY HEART, LEFT OPEN AND FESTERING.*

3. My age spots on my cheeks worry me. I try to be high-minded about what they show to the world about a life fully lived in sunshine and years, but really? How seriously do I have to take that pep talk? Because I have mottled blotches on my cheeks and they tick me off. I am shallow and I want to be cute, and the blotches are messing with my cute.

4. I am often tired. I get to the point every now and then when I ask Marc if he thinks I have a thyroid problem.

---

* I assume you're getting the depth of my issues. A woman should not have gaping wounds because of cupboards.

He has never, ever said yes. First, I am irritated by the fatigue. Second, and much more loudly, I am irritated that Marc is always right and I do not have a thyroid problem. Not *yet*.

5. When our mini schnauzer barks, I cuss. His bark is piercing and shrill and it scares the living daylights out of me. I silence the Holy Spirit and I say a bad word because the dog barks. I keep telling my family that I have unusually sensitive hearing and that the dog's bark physically hurts me. They ignore me because THEY ARE TOO BUSY DROPPING EIGHTY-SEVEN PAIRS OF SHOES BY THE BACK DOOR AND CANNOT BE BOTHERED.

When I think about my grandma, I do not think of her wrestling with these things. I think of her corralling a bunch of marginally talented church members every year for the Easter pageant. I'm not trying to be difficult, but I don't imagine her town of fifteen hundred people had a deep bench in the thespian department. Still, she got it done every year, marching farmers and accountants and librarians to moving performances and stage makeup and memorized lines.

I think of her going to Israel in her fifties and mounting a camel as if it were just like the horses on her childhood farm.

I think about her willingness to dive into spirited conversations up to the very end. Being spirited in all things was big with Edna, even with her choice of footwear. Edna, actually, probably would have contributed to the shoe problem in my house because she loved her cute feet and had an Imelda-Marcos-level collection. But she wouldn't have stressed out about a pile of them and the need to pole-vault over them every time I walked by. She would probably sing with wild vibrato as she grabbed the pole.

IF MY GRANDMA could read these pages, I am certain she would frown and say I was only telling part of the story, that she had plenty of faults, and perhaps I'd like to hear about some of them? I have the tendency to make all my heroes into giants, and I'd guess you do too. We are on the hunt for heroes, so we make them out of people who are just, well, people. Sometimes those giants seem untouchable. Sometimes the folks who look like they have it all make the rest of us wonder at our own sanity, our own gritty earthiness, our own struggles to build anything valuable and lasting when all we feel like we do every day is scream at the dog and pick up shoes.

Jesus was really good at kicking that myth in the shins. He looked at our giant-ranking system and said it was bunk. The giants in first-century Galilee, the people with the fancy religious pedigrees and nice clothes, those guys, He said out loud, were actually the scoundrels. The insides of their hearts were dark and dirty and needed a thorough power-washing renovation, He said. And then He used the simplest language to make spiritual truths normally commandeered by the giants seem accessible to poor people and outcasts and train wrecks and women, for goodness' sake. Women, who weren't supposed to even speak with their husbands in public, much less allowed to engage in talking about the character of God.

Jesus made the power brokers nervous because He knew their rules were ridiculous at best and God-disrespecting at worst.

Jesus used his own carpentry-calloused hands to touch lepers, shocking everybody, both the lepers with their palpable hunger for connection and the fake giants. He scandalized the whole bunch with His brazen disregard for the cogs that kept their machine humming along. One by one, Jesus removed the cogs and the machine limped and lurched and finally sputtered out altogether, right outside an unmarked, empty grave.

Jesus kept after the average, the regulars, the ordinary, the train wrecks, the brokenhearted, and He kept looking them in the eye, kept touching their ravaged bodies, kept peeling back the layers of insecurity and hope and anger and curiosity. He kept reaching for the people who could find easy traction in stories about lost sheep and good shepherds and deadbeat sons and good fathers and about all of us losing the way on our trek to find God. He knew that the real heroes are busy living full-tilt in the direction of the One who made them, and that a life lived in that direction is beautiful, whether it's in first-century Palestine or on a tulip-lined street in a small town in Iowa.

He and Edna were in full agreement on that point.

I HAD THE honor of being with my Grandma Edna the last week of her full-tilt life. I held her hand, touched her cool cheek, reminded her that she was safe and fiercely loved. I cried with her and I laughed with her and I asked God over and over to give me what I needed to walk this patch of road well.

And then I did all those things again.

That last week or so felt like we had entered some strange space where time stretched like a slow-pour ribbon of molasses, like the seconds weren't actually ticking off but that the numbers were stuck, immovable. The first days were filled with lots of Grandma as I knew her: laughing her contagious laugh, even if it was weaker than her normal; asking for her berry-wine lipstick for a refresher coat; wondering where her crossword was or if her hair was just too terrible since she hadn't had it "set." But she wasn't eating well. She wasn't sleeping more than a few minutes at a time. She was becoming confused and would say the same things over and over, as if her brain, wicked sharp up until those last strides around the track, was now betraying her and she was trying to tame it into submission.

I hadn't known that dying is hard work.

Her body was letting her down at every turn, so it was a little startling to me when I could glimpse her healthy spirit. For a while she got stuck on the prayer, "Thank you, Lord, for your grace and your mercy." She said it over and over, without pause. "Thank you, Lord," pause, rattled breath, "for your grace and your mercy." Then she would stop and close her eyes, only to start up again. Grace and mercy. Grace and mercy. Her spirit was stubborn in its memory, even as her body refused to do her bidding.

She was struggling to remember conversations we were in the middle of navigating, but she could remember every word of every hymn as soon as I began to sing. We sang all four verses, and I had never been so grateful to be the oddball who loved poetry and language and all four verses of songs no one sang anymore. I was ready for this part, my old soul comfortable with tested words and melodies. Grandma kept up without a hitch. Even phrases like "Sun, moon and stars in their courses align," and "Join with all nature in manifold witness," and "Here I raise my Ebenezer—" She nailed them all, perfectly on pitch. She would watch my face, my mom's face, my aunts' faces as we sang, unperturbed by the tears streaming down our cheeks and our wobbly voices. She would keep singing and nod, as if she was remembering all the times she had sung those songs and had dared God to show her that the words were true.

The words were true.

That really odd phrase, "Here I raise my Ebenezer," means "thus far the Lord has helped me." An Ebenezer stone is a big rock that's set up with the intention to remind a person or a family of a time that God helped them through. A time when He fought a battle for them that they were never going to win on their own.

The longer I walk with my heart fixed on grace, the more Ebenezer stones I want to put up. My life is littered with those stones. Marker upon marker of when God fought a battle for me I couldn't possibly fight on my own. Entire roadways paved with stones of remembrance, reminders that grace is enough in all the spaces I am not. Grace cushions the hard falls. Grace takes our hands and leads us Home.

AT ONE POINT during those last days with Grandma, I was alone with her in her room when she took my hands in hers. Her eyes were wide as they searched mine.

"Am I dying?" she asked. Her voice was worn and rough. Her fingers felt papery and cool in mine.

My throat constricted and my heart began to race, but I tried to answer how she had taught me, looking life straight in the face and telling the truth.

"Grandma, I think you are."

I immediately winced at the sound of those words cutting into the quiet. I wondered if I should have distracted or delayed or just not answered at all. My mom should be the one to say this, I thought. Or someone else, someone more qualified. I'm just a grandkid. I'm just here for the hugs.

Grandma closed her eyes and sat back in her chair. She sighed, relief flooding her face. "I've almost finished my race."

I was crying and didn't respond. I didn't need to. Grandma was raising her final Ebenezer, a final battle cry to the One who fought the most important fights for her. A race run to the very last stretch with an eye on what would make it a race worth running. It wasn't a perfect race. It wasn't a race without a limp, false starts, stutter steps. But it was, as Eugene Peterson wrote, long obedience in the same direction.

Grace and mercy. Grace and mercy. That's what remained when everything else faded away. And it's what will remain for us too.

PART IV

OUT THERE

MAYBE EVERY GENERATION DESPAIRS OF THE lunacy it faces. Lunacy in the public square, the school system, the home, the church...There are all sorts of ways these places drive us nuts and make us reach for a blankie, some chocolate, and a good novel. Or maybe that's just me.

Unless you live in an underground bunker (in which case, please help me understand this life choice), you have likely noticed that people are real darn difficult these days. And they are loud about their difficult-ness. The ways in which other people can get under our skin are myriad and astonishing and very, alarmingly easy, accessible even as they wait in line for coffee. An extra gigantic latte with oat milk and vanilla and a sprinkle of cinnamon and nutmeg, please, and also I vehemently oppose your politics/hairstyle/feelings/worldview/choice of pet. Send. That will be five dollars and eighteen cents.

Oh, I also oppose coffee inflation.

Like, dislike, love, indignant exclamation points.

The world is parched for grace. We need it everywhere. We need it far more than we need to share our opinions or debate our opinions or hold fast to our opinions. We need grace more than we need to be right all the time, and we need grace more than we need to defend, oppose, or fully embrace. We need grace like we need deep gulps of air after long stretches of swimming under-water. Grace gives us a clear head and a light spirit, both of which are in short supply on any given Tuesday.

The grace that sets us free will set our people free too. When we start breathing it in as a regular practice, we realize that not only did we not earn even one tiny bit of the grace that's changing us, we also cannot possibly keep it all to ourselves. Grace roots in hearts and then it runs like a river out there, in the wild, in the disarray and the despair and noise. And because God loves to turn every table upside down, we are the ones who get to be the unqualified couriers. We get to see grace in action, join grace in action.

Grace is weighty, and it's powerful. It can change a life and change a room, and it can also change a world.

STAY IN YOUR LANE

I RAN TRACK IN JUNIOR HIGH AND HIGH SCHOOL. IT was a poor decision. I have what we will diplomatically call an athletic build. It confuses people. I look like I should be able to do something with my, ahem, strong legs. My dad's calves, for example, should be worth something.

My dad has given me some really wonderful things. For example, he taught me how to jump a car in the dead of an Iowa winter. He taught me how to floss. He taught me how to love people and God well with generous hands and that our goal is to slide into Home with super-empty pockets and super-full hearts.

Those are really lovely gifts. I'm grateful. I am.

If I could just be picky, however, and how can I not when I am a firstborn female, I would have liked not to receive his calves.

I want my mom's calves. My mom's calves are cute and feminine and cheerleader-y.

My dad's calves helped him land a full-ride college football scholarship. The calves are like entities unto themselves. They have girth. They are wider than many thighs, and that's not exactly the proportion I'm going for.

My calves are Randy calves.

Once when I got a pedicure, I wore skinny jeans and could get them up but not down. The pedicurist was sweating as he tried to unroll my jeans back over my Randy calves. Picture that, if you will. The poor man sprouted beads of sweat on his forehead because of my calves. I assured him I loved capris and not to worry about it and to just take a breather with some lemonade before his next appointment. He deserved the recovery. I left the salon with my feet stuffed in those pretend flip-flops, toes looking fantastic, calves bared like two muscular weapons, and jeans bunched up around my knees.

It was a defeating moment.

My junior high track coach knew my dad and that he was an accomplished athlete, so she convinced me to try out for track. When I say "try out," I mean "show up." Our track team was so small, we all had to participate in roughly eight events per runner. And when I say "runner," in my case, I mean "jogger and wheezer."* We all had to do everything. In one meet, I promise I ran the open 100, the 4 x 100, the open 200, and the 4 x 200; I

---

* I complained about not being able to breathe all through track, every year. In college, I was diagnosed with asthma. So I would like to take this opportunity to shame my parents, particularly my SUPER-ATHLETIC DAD, who said each time I would showcase my breathing, all red-cheeked and crackly lungs, "Sounds like you need to do some more conditioning." The revenge of writers is real, nerdy girls everywhere. Take heart.

threw shot put; I did the long jump; and I ran hurdles. Coach Em took me out to the middle of the oval and put a hurdle in front of me, saying, "Just try it. We'll get points for participation."

When I looked at her with fear in my eyes, she jogged away in her track suit and low-maintenance haircut and said, "You're up in ten minutes!"

I blame my calves for this entire misunderstanding. They distracted Coach Em from the truth, which is that her real hope would be coming down the pike in my brother and sister, both of whom would be college athletes. My calves were like decoys. They looked like I should be able to sprint. They were really muscular fibbers.

EVEN THOUGH I wasn't a fast runner, I did enjoy the way running made me feel emptied out when I was finished.* I ran for years, long after I'd convinced my track coaches I was Randy's daughter but only because of genetics, not because of ability. Running became something I could do anywhere, as long as I had some basic gear and a little time. I started to think I was pretty good at it when I wouldn't collapse at the end. Not collapsing was my one and only rubric for running success. I was pretty sure at that point that I looked vaguely Olympian when running. I'm sure you've seen those ripped runners on TV? The ones that have miraculously shaped butts and wear jewelry and do their nails because when you run that fast, you automatically look like a goddess so you might as well adorn yourself? I thought I looked

---

* Especially after I got my hands on an inhaler. THANKS FOR NOTHING, DAD.

like that when I ran. I thought maybe I should even find Coach Em to say I forgave her for forcing me to hurdle. Running as an adult was totally different. I was pretty much fantastic at it.

And then I saw myself running in a video.

I did not look Olympian.

I looked like a sloth. In Lycra. With a limp. And unfortunate bangs. Who'd accidentally taken a tranquilizer called Go Slower.

After that video, I never quite found the same jolt of happiness with my running. Okay, I was never exactly jolting with happiness, but before the video, I had thought I was doing pretty well. After the video, I knew I did not look the part and so I probably just wasn't. That video reminded me of every junior high track meet when I would line up next to The Fast Girls dressed in fancy shoes, their sleek, long legs dead ringers for antelopes, and possessing not one nervous bone in their bodies. I would be scouting out the nearest place to toss my cookies while The Fast Girls would be doing little dances on the asphalt, brushing off crumbs from the Krispy Kremes they'd just mowed down. They ate *donuts* before running and still won every race, while my Chihuahua legs and I slogged across the finish line, dead last and pining for albuterol.

Here's one way to wreck your experience with grace: Pay attention to the person in the next lane. Keep track of their pace, their gait, their time, how they look when they're running their race. Do that for long and you won't only make your race harder, you'll forfeit something beautiful. You'll give it up for something cheaper. Something flimsy. Something that's worthless and that steals your life.

This reminds me of a woman named Rosie. Rosie ran the Boston Marathon in 1980, and she won the female division.

She didn't just win it. She conquered it. She won with a time of 2 hours, 31 minutes, 56 seconds, the third-fastest recorded time for any female marathon runner to that point. She ran 26 miles in the time it takes me to watch three episodes of *The West Wing*, a feat I have perfected and which doesn't make me sweat hardly at all.

Rosie really wasn't that sweaty, either. She'd crossed the finish line looking strong, this surprise-hit rock star of the field, unknown to the rest of the running world until that point. And do you know how she did it? Do you know how this petite fireball raced to the end and left interviewers breathless with shock?

She skipped most of the race.

Rosie jumped into the throng about a mile away from the finish line. She thought she was joining somewhere near the middle of the pack, but she ended up being the first female to cross the line.

This was Rosie's second hurrah at faux-marathon-running. A few months earlier, she'd hopped on the subway during the New York City Marathon but later said she'd finished. The subway was a good break, but she didn't mention that part.

My guess is that Rosie had checked out the races of other runners and decided her version couldn't match up. So she cheated. She totally missed running her own race. She cheapened the whole gig because she didn't stay in her lane. She got the laurel wreath on her not-sweaty head, and she got to keep the medal, but it wasn't worth anything. In fact, the medal and the wreath just mocked her in the end. They were pretend prizes for a pretend race she ran on the subway and for only the very last mile.

I don't want this for us. I don't want us to miss our own beautiful, broken, messy, triumphant adventures because our heads are on swivels and we are looking to the left, to the right, checking out what the girl or guy in the next lane is up to. I don't want us to miss what we are wired to live because we are too busy fussing about why we don't have what is one lane over.

There's this great scene in the Bible where a man named Nehemiah is rebuilding the wall around Jerusalem after years of neglect. These trolls keep bugging him, yelling at him that he's a loser, tattling on him to their boss. They are relentless, even trying to attack Nehemiah and his crew to get them to stop. And Nehemiah, the originator of beast mode, says to these jokers, "I am doing a great work and I can't come down." I AM BUSY. Stay in your own lane, chumps, and I will stay in mine. I am doing something great here. My guess is that it looks like a lost cause to you. My guess is that you think I should do something else, something more to your liking, maybe something more polite or less disruptive. Something that makes you feel better about your own aimlessness. Listen: I'm not asking you to understand it, Nehemiah says. I'm just telling you how it is.

I'm doing a great work. I am busy. I am not coming down to your lane because then I'd have to leave mine.

My friend Makila says this in another way: CBB. Can't Be Bothered.

I wholeheartedly recommend that you try this. Text it the next time someone sends you a passive-aggressive message or tells you a story that only cuts down and doesn't build up or asks you to be less, do less than you are. Text or say or email back, "CBB." You can pretend later that you had a weird hand twitch and those are nonsense syllables. But secretly you'll know.

CBB. Can't be bothered with envy for where you are and where I am not. Can't be bothered with trying to inch my way into your lane when my lane has really great work for me to do, right where I am.

☆ ☆ ☆

THE PRESSURE TO lane-drift is intense. It starts early. Pre-school is a rough estimate.

Mitch's preschool put together this magical, adorable little Christmas program each year. This was a good fit because, at age four, Mitch was also magical and adorable. He was fully out of the phase where he tossed my cell phone in the toilet,* and he hadn't quite entered the part where he "didn't hear" me when I'd ask him to do a chore or come downstairs now-and-not-in-five-minutes for dinner. He also had a crop of white-blond hair, eyes the color of cornflowers, and he wore these ridiculously cute black-rimmed glasses. It was a golden era.

The program began, and the kids filed onto the steps in front of pews crammed with eager parents. This was a golden era for parents as well. We didn't yet associate our progeny's school programs with the soul-sucking exercises that waited just around the bend. Efficiency Expert Marc would want you to know that preschool programs clocked in at a respectable thirty minutes or fewer. Marc has never gotten over the shock of one high school choir concert that languished for two hours and forty-five minutes, so for him, the preschool program situation educes longing and nostalgia.

Rows of these unjaded parents whipped out their cameras and balanced them while waving back at their children. Again,

---

* I threw his beloved blue stuffed dog, Johnny, into the bowl after my phone. It was an effective strategy. We never had to revisit that particular lesson again.

the golden age. Later, I would witness one of these same children pretend she had suddenly gone both deaf and blind when her mother tried to talk with her in the lobby after a freshman orchestra concert. That child on this preschool program day waved so enthusiastically at her parents, they had to make a motion to dial it back so she didn't injure her rotator cuff.

Marc and I usually arrived late enough to walk in with the performers.* That day, however, we staked out our front row spots early, and we grinned at Mitch when he walked in with his classmates, geared up in his argyle vest and white oxford shirt.

The music started and here is where we hit a snag.

As soon as the chipper intro of "Joy to the World" ended and the kids started to sing along, Mitch lifted his hands just below his chin, cocked his wrists, pointed his fingers downward, and pulled back his upper lip to expose his teeth as he sang. He sang every word. He knew them all, and he sang them through his mouth that he had contorted to look like a woodchuck. A woodchuck that was fond of hand choreography.

Marc watched, mouth slightly parted, body perfectly still. I lasted about thirty seconds and I started to laugh those heaving, socially inappropriate guffaws that only happen during church and funerals. The ones that take over one's body in an effort to escape, thereby rendering the laugher herself useless to stop anything at all. When "Joy to the World" ended, Mitch put his hands at his sides, smiled at the audience, acted as if all was totally well with his world. Then "Silent Night" started up, and I thought

---

* We have also entered weddings with the bridal party. Don't invite us to your wedding. Or if you must, please scratch out the real time on the invite and bump it up a half hour. It's in everyone's best interests.

that Mitch, now in the introspective part of the program, would stop with the rodent thing and just sing like the other kids. Mitch is our middle child. He barely has a pulse. He does not seek the limelight or the spotlight or even a flashlight. He just assumes it will all work out, and he's pretty much always right. This Star Search moment was distinctly unlike him in every regard.

Turns out, the rodent was introspective.

Mitch kept up the choreography and the retracted lip/buck teeth for every single song. Every tempo, every tone, songs about Jesus and songs about snowmen. They were all fair game, and they all got a little special touch from the chill middle child.

Our video recording of this experience is toast. I gave up. I had to ask my friend, Ann, for a copy because her husband managed to keep it together while Ann and I died a million, laughter-seizure deaths and Marc just sat there, looking pained and confused to the fiber of his introvert being.

"What is he doing?" he whispered, face frozen, eyes glued to his son, who was supposed to be the nonperformer in a house full of loud women.

"I really don't know," I choked out between snorts of laughter.

Ann was in a coma.

When the kids and teachers filed down the center aisle, Mrs. Grey, Mitch's teacher, leaned in as she walked by.

"I'm not sure what that was all about," she said, all kindness in a way only preschool teachers can speak. They are made of different material than the rest of us. She shook her head in wonder. "He didn't do that during our rehearsal."

When Marc asked him about it later, Mitch acted just a little sheepish as he shrugged. He had no answer. Not one word to explain why he had suddenly put on his inner Cher (or wildlife expert) when all eyes were on him. Marc seemed satisfied that Mitch wasn't going to make this a habit, and indeed, Mitch has never returned to the woodland animal repertoire in scores of choir and orchestra concerts since. But I knew what was going on. I knew it because I've done it myself. Mitch was suddenly and acutely aware that people were watching. He realized there were a lot of lanes to choose from, and against his better judgment, he decided that for a very public half hour, he would pretend to be someone he was not.

Mitch just needed to be himself. That's all we were looking for. He didn't need to jazz anything up or drape himself in tinsel or add some sweet moves to the simple song he was singing. We just wanted the song and his voice, no bells, no whistles. We just wanted him.

Junior high and junior high track are only good for one go-around. We don't need to keep checking out what's going on in the lane next to us. It doesn't even matter if the people who share the track are running faster than us or slower than us, if they look really cute in their track suits or if they had better luck than we did, clearing that last hurdle. What matters is that we run the race unfolding right in front of us. We don't even need to freak out about the final 100 meters. The few that will meet our feet this week are good enough.

I don't want to get to the end of this gig and realize that all I got out of it was a really keen awareness of how everyone else was running. I want to finish the race only I get to run, and I want that for you too. I want to be one of a beautiful, motley cohort of runners, walkers, limpers, and dancers who move with freedom and abandon through this world. I want to be the girl who shrugs at the distractions, the naysayers, the spotlight chasers and flashes a "CBB" instead. Can't be bothered, folks. I have some great work to do, and the really good news is that I can't— nope, I won't—come down.

WORDS

MY CHILDREN SAY SO, SO MANY WORDS IN A GIVEN day. They are all verbal processors. Every last one of them.

I know what you're thinking, and you are wrong. This is not my fault. People often make this mistake, so don't beat yourself up, but this is all Marc's doing. He says he's an introvert. Okay, fine, but I'm only going with that if introverts can be super chatty.

Marc is super chatty, just not in public. He saves all his chatty for our home. In fact, we have a theme song for this. It's called the "Marcky Report." We sing it to the tune of the Octonauts' theme song.* Marc has some issues with wanting to be more productive than what is natural for humans. He makes lists with seventy to eighty items per weekend, and then he feels like a moral failure if he only completes sixty-eight of them. He's working on not being absolutely (a) hospital-grade tired every day of his life and (b) psycho, but at the time of this writing, the pull of a robust task list remains strong.

One way Marc deals with this productivity obsession is to give me book reports every evening on all the things he's accomplished. I didn't realize this was hilarious until recently when Mitch came into our room right before bed. Marc was full-throttle into his report and barely paused when his son entered.

"And then I returned some zip ties to Home Depot, where I saw that there were some light bulbs on sale, so I bought fourteen packages. And then I called Don our accountant about our tax return because I had some questions. He wasn't there but I left a message with his assistant, Loreen."

Mitch watched Marc for a while, sitting quietly while Marc moved on from Loreen to his afternoon appointment with his orthodontic patient who had a really tough case and a mom who was, in his diplomatic language, "challenging." In my diplomatic language, I translated to Mitch that the mom was "a nutjob."

Mitch nodded, eyes on Marc as he bulldozed through a story about fixing a piece of lab equipment.

---

* *The Octonauts* is an animated program my kids used to watch. It features animals with really round heads running around the marine world and then coming back to share their research in a "Creature Report." I would guess this show aired on public television since Marc and I were total cultural snobs for a couple minutes before parenting made us too exhausted to care if our kids learned anything, ever.

"What is he doing?" Mitch spoke quietly and tipped his chin at Marc.

I tucked my feet under the covers and fluffed my pillow. "Oh, he's giving his report."

Mitch wrinkled his forehead. "Does he do this often?"

"Every night," I said, trying to signal to both of the verbal processors in the room that now was my time to read a novel. Short responses, no eye contact.

It never works.

"Dad," Mitch said loudly.

Marc paused, midsentence, snapped out of his productivity trance. He focused on Mitch's face. "Hi, buddy."

Mitch laughed his big, rolling laugh. "Love the reporting, Dad. It's super comprehensive."

Marc smiled. "Thank you!" Check that box. Comprehensive reporting. Done, and *nailed* it. Next!

Even if you don't have to endure the Marcky Report every night *when you just want to be by yourself and read two paragraphs of a story about fake people before you go to sleep*, you, too, are inundated with words. We all are. Our news feeds, the never-ceasing storm of social media, TV, podcasts, all the people who share your gene pool—we can't escape the barrage. We hear a lot and we say a lot.

Should we look at the data? Normally, I feel data are big fat boring. I was not a stats major.

Any stats majors out there?

Why did you do that?

Anyway, data are usually not super fun, but I found some that are. There's this psychologist named Matthias Mehl, and he conducted a study to see if the stereotype is true: Do women really use more words in a day than men? I asked Marc to weigh in on this question, and he wisely responded in the manner that always wins: I was just thinking about how you look particularly beautiful lately.*

It turns out that men and women say the same number of words a day. The average person speaks 16,000 words a day, men and women alike. That's the average. I do feel the need to point out that both the top talker in Matthias's study and the least talkative person studied were men. Top Talker spoke 47,000 words in a single day, assumedly some in the ER when his wife went in with bleeding ears. And the most taciturn was a gentleman who spoke only 700 words in a single day. I know Jesus tells me to love everybody, but can someone else volunteer to host Mute Man for dinner? Seven hundred words IN TOTAL? I can squeeze that number of words in before I get out of bed in the morning. I'm not the target market for Mute Man, so can I get a hard pass on two hours of silent chewing?

Notwithstanding the outliers, the average person speaks about 16,000 words a day. I have helpful comps:

- The Bible contains 783,137 words. This count is from the King James version of the Bible, which is very difficult to understand unless you work at Renaissance fairs. It's also famously minimalist, so this number is probably lower in comparison to other, more readable versions of the Bible. Tack on an extra 10K if we're talking about *The Message* paraphrase, for example,

---

* Marc was not a stats major, but he knows how to be careful with data collection.

the version that is very readable and includes a recipe for s'mores in the appendix.

- *War and Peace* by Tolstoy: 587,287 words. This book can also double as a patio paver.
- *Sugar* by Kimberly Stuart: ~80,000 words. In addition to this being a shameless plug for one of my novels, I sweated out every one of those words, so I'm planting a flag on this one. Eighty thousand words is pretty average for a contemporary novel, at least in the rom-com genre.[*]

At 16,000 words a day, that means the average person speaks 112,000 words a week.

We speak a novel and a half every week.

And here's the question I have to ask myself and maybe one you should ask yourself too: What kind of story are we writing with our words?

☆ ☆ ☆

I AM PERPETUALLY astonished at how quickly I can down this plane. Often I do it before 9 a.m. Marc, as usual, is a better human in this regard. Sure, his Marcky Reports aren't going to win any literary prizes for inventiveness. But they are humane. Marc uses words to chronicle, not to maim. I can maim.

I have a really long history of using my words to injure. I think I realized this about myself for the first time when I was about fifteen. My brother, Ryan, was around twelve at the time,

---

[*] It's like *Sleepless in Seattle* meets the Food Network! You'll love it!

and he was suddenly taller and stronger than I was. I remember the morning in our kitchen on Patricia Drive when I stared at him, narrowing my eyes over my bowl of Grape Nuts, and it occurred to me that my days of being able to pummel him were over forever. No more pummeling. I would have to use my words to inflict harm.* Ryan could pick me up and tote me to another room, and I was powerless to protest. Usually the toting was in fun, but if it ever turned into something I wanted to control, if I ever wanted to squirm out of a head lock, my only weapon was my voice. Take down his girlfriend with a cruel remark. Comment on his unruly cowlick that day. Make him feel small, even at 200 pounds of myth-worthy muscle.

He'd drop me from his playful grip, face fallen, walk away without a word.

There's an old proverb that says the tongue holds the power of life and death. *Life and death.* Both of those things, fully held in one, tiny muscle. I can say words that will blossom into life and green shoots of renewal and restoration, bringing whole things from broken ones. Or with that same mouth, I can tug a person down into a pit, convince them to stay there, bury them with unkindness, defeat, or the worst of all, the cold slap of indifference.

My mouth can do that.

My mouth is a peace treaty and a nuclear weapon, all at once.

Versailles and Hiroshima, in the very same breath.

I suspect I'm not alone in this, but my targets of choice are usually the people I love the most. I can sling grenades with my mouth in our living room and then answer the door to a neighbor

---

* Perhaps now is the best time to apologize to Ryan and to my sweet sister, Lindsay, for the years 1988 to the present.

and sound like Julie Andrews. It's appalling. My kids have looked at me like I grew an extra head when I've gone from screaming about a dirty kitchen to answering my phone in my maple syrup voice.

"Hi, friend!" I gush, over the sniffles of my children. "It's so good to hear from you! How *are* you?"

Liar, liar, maple syrup pants on fire.

☆ ☆ ☆

WHAT I REALLY need is a bark collar.

Have you heard of these things? We have one. It gave me my life back.

Our mini schnauzer, Scout, has his merits. For one, he's relatively cute. His cuteness apex occurred when he was a puppy, so there has been a downward slide, but still. Scout is pretty cute.

Another merit is that Scout thinks I am Jesus. Like the actual Jesus. When I come into a room, he comes close to self-injury, he's so excited to see me. When I leave, he stands by the door and looks at the seam between door and doorframe, waiting for my second coming, sure it will happen but just praying it will happen really soon. And when it does, even if I've just stepped into the garage to take out the trash, I reenter to leaping and dancing and sounds that would probably be joy weeping if Scout were human.

So Scout has his perks. One of his less winsome habits, though, is his bark. It is shrill. It is piercing. It has, and I'm not kidding, caused me to lose control of my bladder on more than one occasion.*

---

*   I have birthed three children.

This needed to stop or Scout was going to be "relocated" to a "farm" where "other children" could "enjoy him" and he could "run and play forever."

Enter the bark collar. This thing is remarkable. When Scout barks, it sprays a little puff of citronella. Citronella, apparently, is repulsive to mini schnauzers. Or maybe to Germans. I can't really worry about the details of why; I just know that the bark collar allows Scout to be who he needs to be, which is a relatively cute dog who is obsessed with me, and I can be who I need to be, which is a dog owner who doesn't lose her ever-loving mind every time a squirrel sashays by our window.

I need a bark collar for my own self. I need a little nudge to think before I speak. Think before I pierce. Think before I shrill. Think before I drive the people around me to want to take me to "a farm."

Sometimes the novel I've written with my weekly word count has been one about an entitled, cranky, selfish girl who should have taken a vow of silence for that particular seven-day stretch.

But here's something beautiful: Remarkably, when I pull those novels off the shelf and bring them, shamefaced and sorry, to my family to apologize for past wrongs, I find they didn't stick. My kids, Marc, those dearest to me, they might remember the scene in which I lost my mind and used my mouth like something out of *Hunger Games*, but they often shrug and say, "It's okay. I totally forgive you. In fact," they often add, "I'd forgotten you even said that."

I wonder if they are telling the truth or if they're just trying to make me feel better about the many ways my words have slashed through our relationships over the years. Or maybe they are just trying to skate past it all, forget it, not talk about it so we can lessen the sting.

I've watched these people I love, though. I watched these people who love me, and I think they are saying the truth. I think those old words are true, that love really does cover a multitude of sins, even when the sinner keeps dragging dark things into the light to poke and prod them to make sure they really are dead and they really won't hurt us anymore. Love covers that stuff up. It takes hard memories and bruised hearts and holds them in the same hand, then shrugs and says, "I totally forgive you."

The real stuff, real, true, tenacious love looks at a person's body of work, not just that one subpar novel no one really liked and that only sold a few copies. The book that wasn't my best? The one with the unconvincing protagonist and the one-dimensional villain and the plot that was a total snooze-fest? The stubborn love I've lived with my family doesn't keep that book around, even if there are a lot of unsold copies.

"That book?" my kids say.

"That one with the broken spine?" Marc asks.

"Oh, right." They nod and furrow their brows, as if trying to place a memory. "I'd forgotten you'd even written that."

The body of work is what remains. It's the sum of our parts that sticks. If you've downed your plane today, pick through the wreckage, take anything worth salvaging, and hug everyone who witnessed the crash. Tell them you are sorry for your abysmal piloting skills. Hold their faces in your hands and look them in the eye and tell them you love them in a way that the flames behind you do not reflect. Your love for them is strong and wide and deep, and you're going to get right back to showing them that story instead of the disaster right behind you.

The people who love you will hear your words and they'll feel you hugging them with both arms as you move away from the mess. They'll share the next meal with you, hover over cups of coffee with you the next morning, walk the dog with you in the afternoon. And as you keep calling mayday and you keep saying sorry and you keep writing new stories, those people will really only remember your body of work, the whole shelf full, not just a page here and there where the hero failed in an epic and kamikaze way. You'll wince when you think of those pages, but if you bring them up, the people who have been reading all your words over many years will look at you, cock their heads to one side as they sift through their stacks of memories. And then they'll shake their heads, tell you they have no idea what you're talking about, and wonder if we can bake cookies and eat them for dinner.

And you'll answer that of course we can.

Because we are writing a novel here, and the best novels make you want to always and loudly and forever say "yes."

LEAST LIKELY

MY DAD USED TO WEAR SUITS A LOT. IT WAS HIS thing. He wore them to work, even though he was a dentist. These were the years before plagues, and though now he wears scrubs Monday through Friday, for many years he wore a suit and tie. He thought it made him look more professional under his white lab coat. My mom probably thought that blood from people's incisors hampered that look, but she knew which battles to fight, and suits and ties were off the list.

My dad wore a suit to work, and he wore a suit to church on Sundays. Dad is the eldest of five kids and was the first in his family to finish college. My grandparents weren't able to schlep him back and forth from university every time he made a trip home. So when it was time to get back to school after a weekend home, Dad would put on his brown plaid suit and his dress shirt with the butterfly collar, walk out to the highway on the edge of his small town, and hitchhike a ride across the state.

Suits were his uniform. He wasn't super motivated to change out of them at the end of the day, mostly because he was always in motion and changing clothes required something of a pause. My mom had to do deep yogic breathing fairly frequently when she would come upon my dad, newly home from work and painting a wall or sloshing windshield wiper fluid into his car or building a deck, all still in his suit. My dad wore a suit to work, he wore a suit to church on Sundays, and he wore a suit when he was going door to door with a group from his Bible study, telling people about heaven, hell, and Jesus.

I realize this puts my dad in an uncomfortable category shared with cult members and people in airports with whom we must, we *must* avoid eye contact. I understand your worries when you envision a man in a suit, making his way up and down residential streets, clutching a Bible and ready to ask you how you feel about your eternal prospects. I was probably really uncomfortable about this idea in college. I was uncomfortable about most ideas in college. But now I know that Dad is just wired to talk to people about real things. He is really, horribly bad at small talk. Here's a sample conversation over dinner:

Me: Good gravy, is this a beautiful day or what?! We made it through another Iowa winter!

Dad: Today a gal came into the office. She needed a root canal but didn't have any money, so we just gave it to her.

Her boyfriend is a loser, and I think he's gotten rough with her, so I walked her out to the lobby and stayed there while she dumped him and then found her an apartment for the next year. She prayed to receive Christ and is now running for public office. Great pork. Pass the potatoes.

It only makes sense that Dad would continue these conversations in a suit on neighborhood streets. He didn't seem at all worried about looking foolish or saying the wrong thing. He wasn't hanging his hat on anyone's response, either. If you wanted to surrender to Jesus, that would be wise. And if you didn't, he'd catch you later. Pass the potatoes.

On one of these outings, Dad came to Freda's house. She answered the door, hair set in neat curls, the bright white waves tinged light blue. She peered through the small slit in the door she was offering to this stranger, but even with the limited view, Dad could see that she'd been crying. He introduced himself and asked her about her tears.

"Today is my wedding anniversary," Freda said, her lower lip shaking with a new wash of grief. "My husband John died three years ago, and I suppose I'm feeling sorry for myself."

When Dad came back to her front step an hour later, bearing a bouquet of flowers, that was it. Freda was loyal to him from that day onward.

We picked up Freda for church pretty much every Sunday after that. They had a system, Dad and Freda. The system was that Dad would come downstairs, toweling his hair after a shower, suit on, face nicked in a few places after shaving. He'd say to whoever was in the room and scarfing breakfast, "Anybody call Freda yet?"*

We would sip our orange juice, look at him blankly. We knew our roles in this drama, and we were not responsible for calling The Freedmeister.

Dad would nudge the telephone off its cradle, punch in Freda's number, and say his lines.

Dad: Morning, Freda! You coming to church?

Freda: Oh, I don't know, Randy. I'm not even dressed, and I didn't sleep very well—

Dad: See you in ten! (*Drops phone on cradle and leaves to brush his teeth.*)

The relationship was very uncomplicated.

☆ ☆ ☆

WHEN OUR KIDS were little, Marc and I were mostly just really tired. This might sound whiny, particularly to a Midwestern ear. Midwesterners despise whining. Almost as much as they despise sloth. And spicy food.

The reason we were tired is because young children suck the marrow out of your life until all you have left is an unrelenting eyelid twitch and elaborate, silent fantasies that involve going into a room and closing the door for as long as you want.

---

* This part would vary only in the name Dad used for Freda. "Freed," "The Freedster," and "The Freedmeister" were used in rotation.

Even through the haze of exhaustion, we loved Jesus. Jesus, in fact, was the only one getting us through that stage, so we felt like we owed him. The theology is rough here, but please remember we were tired. Marc and I wanted to find ways to love Jesus by loving other people, but we hit a snag early.

Most of the ways our church helped others involved adults doing adult things, like having deep conversations and using chainsaws and leading small groups. My own children would have had each of those scenarios in flames before everyone had their name tag. Plus, we felt strongly that the church wasn't on the hook to help our kids know how great it was to love people well. We might have had eyelid twitches, but even in our state, Marc and I knew that it was our homework assignment to help our kids know the joy of not thinking about themselves all the ever-loving time.

So we gathered a bunch of our friends and their little kids and met on a Saturday morning and cleaned up the yard of an old house where young girls were getting help they needed in a time they felt alone. There were nine families and roughly three hundred children among us. We were fruitful. We really loved working shoulder to shoulder that Saturday, so we decided to do it again.

A few Saturdays after that, we formed an assembly line and made deli sandwiches for guys who were getting back to work after standing up on shaky legs and battling out of the fog of addiction. It felt sacred to give them something as small but mighty as a lunch because even dragon slayers need a sandwich.

We loved that Saturday, too, so we just kept getting together and coming alongside the good and important work other people in our community had started but couldn't finish by themselves.

We brought bingo cards and a slow cooker full of hot apple cider and we caroled at an apartment building that housed sweet people with canes and walkers and gray hair and decades of stories. We painted cabins at a camp soon to fill with hundreds of teenagers who needed a boost and a reminder that they were strong. We cleared out an overgrown yard at a home where women escape after being sold and used and trafficked. We cried while we ripped out shrubs and weeds, bowed over with grief for what the women had endured and hope for what might be starting to grow in that holy spot.

We called ourselves the Love Corps. Like the Peace Corps, I'd explain, only we shaved our armpits.

I have the tendency to stop before I start. I am really good at thinking about all the ways I won't do something exactly right. The problem is that I'm always correct. I am *not* doing things exactly right. Love Corps was no exception. I bombed it over and over. I said the wrong thing to other families and probably got bossier than they preferred. I never had everything I needed to do all the jobs we tackled. I got us into some scrapes that could have been avoided if I'd been less enthusiastic and more thoughtful.*

I've had this problem from birth, this bent to want to do things perfectly and to protect myself from screwing up by deciding it was safest to wait. Safest to think about it awhile longer. Safest to disqualify myself for service before I've stepped off the front porch. Love Corps forced me to kick that inner editor in

---

* I'm thinking of the morning we cleaned up an abandoned part of our city and I turned to see one of the kids in our group holding a loaded syringe. "Hey, what's this?" he asked before I died eight thousand deaths. That family might still give me the side-eye when I say, "So, I have this idea…"

the teeth, and the beauty our family gleaned from those hours reminds me that sometimes a good teeth-kick is the best possible use of our feistiness.

Less feistiness toward ourselves. More toward loving the things God loves, like justice and mercy and walking humbly with Him through the many briar patches in our neighborhoods and towns.

Exactly no looming societal issues were solved by our chilly mornings mucking garages and putting together meals for hungry people and hanging out with exceptional children while their parents went Christmas shopping. We know who gained the most from those mornings, and it was the broken people who made up our corps. We said the wrong thing sometimes. We worked the wrong way. We screwed up in ways we will never know because the heroes we worked alongside are nice in the way heroes always are.

Even with, maybe especially with, our imperfect efforts, Love Corps was a gift. It was a perpetual object lesson for me that we have what we need to love people well, to let the overflow of grace spill into every space we inhabit. Every Love Corps Saturday when we would leave our houses cranky and thinking of all the neglected items on our own agendas, we'd return a few hours later, full in heart, mind, and spirit, remembering anew what the gift truly was and that we were the grateful recipients. Love Corps taught me that we have enough. That shoulder to shoulder, we are enough. We don't need a program. We *are* the program.

☆ ☆ ☆

FREDA WAS A force. I remember her thumb-wrestling my brother at lunch after church one Sunday. She felt strongly that Ryan was too squirrelly at the table. He was messing with her outing to Bishop's Cafeteria, the restaurant she chose every week and that made me and my siblings quietly groan about in the wayback of the minivan. Ry, Linds, and I were always the youngest diners in Bishop's by one hundred years, probably because we weren't the target market for creamed spinach. So when Ryan let us know he was ready to go at the end of the meal, Freda disagreed on the timing and the expression, and she bent his thumb back toward his wrist. I'm not sure if my parents didn't see this or if they were just grateful to have Freda take a turn with redirecting Ryan's attention, but they said nothing and tucked into another helping of soft foods.

Freda thought my dad was Cary Grant, only better. We mostly agreed and also rolled our eyes because we knew he left his underwear on the floor. She laughed at all his jokes and shook her head, smiling, when he called her The Freedster. She seemed awfully prim to us but would giggle when Dad gave her a hard time or when he helped her step into the minivan by giving her a hand up as if she were climbing a ladder to a tree house. Because she loved my dad, she tolerated his choice of a wife, though she once told my dad under her breath that she was concerned.

"I think Patti is jealous," she said, her eyebrows raised.

My mom felt secure in her marriage, so Freda needn't have worried. My mom ended up being the one who visited Freda the most often, even up to her last days before she died.

The relationship was very uncomplicated.

Freda needed a family. We picked her up for church every week and shared sliced ham and cloverleaf rolls and creamed spinach. We (or at least I as the older sister) felt good about her putting the smack down on Ryan because he needed it and because Freda needed to be needed.

We are all participants in that intricate dance of having a need and helping a need. We live on both sides of the dance floor, and a single step will bridge the divide. We are fully equipped to help each other in the dance. A bouquet of flowers, a minivan with wood paneling, and a few friends who love with abandon—we have all we need. We have the simple things that cross the distance between us.

Let's stop making this tougher than it is.

Don't wait until you feel like you have perfect plans and an empty calendar to move your feet toward people who, like you, are thirsty for grace. The very nature of grace is fluid and wild and in constant motion. Grace doesn't take well to gilded cages. It's meant to give away. And the best part is that we don't have to be ideal messengers. This isn't the Oscars and we only get to deliver good news of this award if we are in a dress or tux with remarkable anti-aging skin. We can wear a suit and bring a bouquet if we want to. Or we can put on our muddy boots and make our way through the woods to tents full of folks who feel invisible.

We have what we need. Lilies of the field get robes, birds of the air get food, and we get all we need to love people well.

What would happen if we really lived like we had enough time, enough energy, enough love and mercy and grace to give them away without constantly counting the cost? I think we would find that even after all the giving, we still have more to go. I think we'd find that beautifully, inexplicably, in the nonsensical economy of grace, we have enough.

NEEDY PEOPLE

RAISE YOUR HAND IF YOU'VE EVER TRIED TO IMPRESS someone. Not raising your hand? Okay, then, raise your hand if you've ever posted on social media. Busted. We love trying to impress each other. The Tower of Babel lives, dear reader. It just lives on a little screen in our pockets. We visit Babel on the regular. For example, the average American spends 147 minutes on social media each day. Apparently we spend an outsized amount of time during our waking hours building our towers and then having open houses.

When we were dating, Marc and I were both on our best, most impressive behavior. He cooked a lot during that heady time. He crafted delicious meals, multiple courses, inspired by his mom, who is an excellent cook, and his love for me, which made him confused and hungrier than normal. For my part, I shaved my legs every day of my life, including above the knee. We wrote countless letters to each other, even when we lived in the same zip code. We competed for Most Declarations of Love in One Phone Call.

These are what we call red herrings. They make a person confident in predictions of the future, but in actuality, they are pump-fakes to real life. Marc didn't cook from the years 2002 to 2020, and that shift only occurred because of a worldwide shut-down. I shave intermittently between Memorial Day and Labor Day. We do write notes to each other, but mostly on Post-it Notes unless it's a national holiday. And while we always, always tell each other we love each other as we hang up the phone, one time this went awry and Marc, so well conditioned, left a message for the manager of his office complex and signed off to A TOTAL STRANGER, "We can talk on Monday. Love ya!"

Sometimes I worry that Jesus followers can get sucked into that new-dating mojo, the idea that we need to impress the world around us. The world values confidence, so we start to think our church experiences had better project confidence. The world prefers neat bows, so we make sure we have those in our speech and our slaps on the back and our chirpy reassurances that things are going great, thanks. The world puts a premium on independence and thinks dependence is weak. And that one infects us too, maybe more dangerously than anything else. We love offering to help but aren't very comfortable receiving any in return. We like to take care of ourselves.

There's just one problem with that. Independence isn't the way of Jesus. Needing God and needing each other is.

I once heard a preacher say you're really never of any use to God until you come to the end of yourself. The end of yourself sounds horrible to me. Like the vacation package of doom. Like the spot on the map you're going to want to avoid, drive around, tell Siri to pick another route.

The last few years, I think we've all glimpsed the end of ourselves. We've seen all the bad things go up, depression, anxiety, violence, division, financial insecurity, while good things, like unity and news stories that don't make us want to crawl back under the covers, go down. I've heard lament, and I've heard folks get angry at the lament. I've seen discord, distrust, and dishonesty, and I've never heard the word "weary" more often in my life.

The end of ourselves has become a neighborhood haunt.

A few weeks ago, I realized I have been waiting for something. I think I've been waiting for the time where everything slots back into what it was before. Let's get back to where we are pretty much in charge. Let's get back to a general sense that we're in control, and we can predict our days, and we sing on Sunday that we need You, God, oh we need You, but actually we prefer not to need You, God. We want to have our need of You be optional. And we would really prefer not to need each other. Needing each other was so early 2020.

I've been feeling like it's time to turn the corner, but I'm learning that the corner is already in the rearview. There's a wonderful curveball here, though, because I'm also learning that we are the keepers of the most countercultural, heartening news for our neighborhoods and our churches and our world. The headline is a stunner. Here it is:

We have come to the end of ourselves.

Huzzah! Throw the ticker tape! Bust out the bubbly! We have come to the end of ourselves, and can we just freaking admit it? Because there is a remedy, closer than the air we breathe. We need Jesus and He came for us! We need the Gospel and God pours it out for us! We need each other because that's the way God made us, to live with and alongside each other, totally, completely NOT self-sufficient.

The end of ourselves is not the pothole we want to avoid. It's the opposite. In fact, the end of yourself, the end of myself, is the most delicious, abundant, freedom-drenched spot to be.

Because the end of ourselves is where we find our not-so-much. It's where we find scrappy grace.

The best faith adventures begin and end with tough, stubborn, scrappy grace, the kind that takes a look at our neediness and runs right into our burning building. I once knew a girl who woke up to find her house on fire. She was a teenager at the time, and while in broad daylight and on a regular snowy Iowa Tuesday, she would never have run out of her house in her PJ T-shirt and shorts, not a stitch of makeup and glasses barely perched on a nose covered with acne cream, you better believe that smoke and flames got that girl to move fast. She did not worry about looking like she was in need of help. She was in desperate need of help.

Our buildings are bursting open with a ten-alarm fire, and the Gospel is made for it. God's favorite currency is one that admits poverty. In fact, Jesus said the poor in spirit are the ones who really get to the good part of the story. It's as if God waits for us to add our names to the Least Likely list hanging by the yearbook office, sees us release the deep breath we didn't even know we'd been holding, and cheers us into a light-filled room.

He delights in finding folks who have nothing left to give and then saying okay, *now* you're ready. Let's go.

☆ ☆ ☆

WHEN MY KIDS were little, they all went through the phase of wanting to do everything by themselves. This happened somewhere after they learned how to walk. Being ambulatory must trigger some outrageous courage in humans because they would quickly transition from utter dependence to utter dependence *with attitude*.

"I do it!" This was the battle cry.

"I do it!" and a lunge for the butter knife.

"I do it!" and an attempt to commandeer the steering wheel of the minivan.

Nobody in that diaper was doing anything. Those children needed help. Their inability to acknowledge their need had nothing to do with their actual need.

God moves when we acknowledge our need of Him. This is the strange economy of Jesus. He is poised at all times to work not through our self-sufficiency but through our poverty, through our need of Him and of each other. The writer of Hebrews says, "Look after each other so that none of you fails to receive the grace of God." What a curious warning. If grace is free and boundless, if the grace of God is infinite, if its vastness is its very nature, it's in no danger of running out. Evidently the only danger is our forgetting to look after each other.

Evidently the gathering in of the grace of God can hit some serious speed bumps when we forget we are in this together.

✩ ✩ ✩

IN ORDER TO do "together" well, we're going to have to admit we need each other. This is going to feel weird, but it really just takes a little practice to nail it.

I grew up in a little red house on a quiet street. We knew all our neighbors. Jim and Louise, who I called Bim and Weeza, had a yard peppered with pretty bird baths. Weeza put a paste of baking soda on my arm one summer day when I got stung by a bee. Our neighbors on the other side were the Tippin family, and they had three girls. Mimi was my age, and we wore down a path in the grass between our houses, we played together so often. Across the street were Kelly and Ben, who were always kind to me and who had an old hound named Spike, who would lie in the middle of our narrow street and wait for cars to go around him, the drivers curbing it and shaking their fists all the way.

When Bim and Weeza moved away, a family of four moved in, and their kids were named Joe and Jeri. My younger brother used those kids as a way to competition-pray with me at the dinner table. Since I was older, I was obviously more spiritual, and I would showcase this important distinction by praying some rather verbose prayers. They lingered. My brother Ryan made up for his deficit in wordiness by praying for Joe and Jeri like this:

"God bless JoeandJeriJoeandJeri..." He would keep one eye open and trained on me. "JoeandJeriJoeandJeri." If I interrupted or protested, reminding my parents that that kind of prayer DID NOT COUNT, my parents hushed me.

"He's learning," they'd say, eyes still closed.

Ryan would grin. I would fume.

We all lived on that quiet street, and alone, we were not-so-much, but together, we were the Pinewood Court family. A colorful family, to be sure. Bim and Weeza were super organized. The kind that vacuumed their garage. Our family was, um, not. Ben was a smoker and Kelly wore tube tops. We didn't. Joe and Jeri's mom and dad owned animal skin rugs, plural, and listened to "Eye of the Tiger" at full volume on Sundays. My dad thought guitar solos had their roots in Hades.

We weren't a lot alike, but we liked each other. We asked each other for help, and we gave help when it was our turn to be on that side of things. We were a motley crew, but it worked.

Listen, I know things have shifted in the neighboring space. These people were my neighbors before the digital age, so I had no idea who Bim and Weeza voted for. I didn't know what Joe and Jeri's mom felt about eating paleo, though judging by the rugs, she felt pretty good about it. I'm not sure if Mimi's dad photoshopped that picture from his niece's wedding or if he was actually pretty bloated that day in Cancún. I didn't know that stuff, and it was awesome. We only knew what came out of actual, real-life conversation.

I don't think those times were perfect, but I think we might be missing something lately. I think we have to learn again how to talk with each other in real time. I think we need to learn how to let our weaknesses be the places where God shows off his redemptive work. I think we need to need each other again. Borrow the sugar. Tell each other when our loved ones have cancer. Confide in each other when we had the best day and the worst one too. Ask each other for help and for conversation on a lonely afternoon, and admit we are tired of praying for our kids.

God bless JoeandJeriJoeandJeri, and may He bless them through our need and our not-so-much.

☆ ☆ ☆

THERE'S A LINE in Matthew's Gospel that says Jesus saw the crowds and had compassion on them because they were harassed and helpless. He knows what we're up against. Jesus sees clearly our need for Him and for each other. He knows we are harassed and helpless and that we need scrappy grace, a grace that plants our feet firmly in the presence of God and holds fast to us, especially in our weakest parts. His power, in fact, is something that only comes to its full, perfect weight when it meets up with our weakness.

How's that for some awe-striking math? His completeness plus our need equals power made perfect. Our wild-eyed running from the burning building, our plaintive confession that all is not, actually, well with our world invites fresh power, set in motion by the only One who can give us grace sufficient.

The world is wrong about weakness, and we have the giddy opportunity to tell it so. Our wounds aren't liabilities after all. Our unsteady steps aren't something to hold us back from better things. Our insecurities and our neediness and our troubled hearts aren't things to cover up. The devastating divorce, the crippling of mind and spirit, the struggle with fill-in-the-blank, the bankruptcy, the still-broken heart—all those things aren't reasons to put on our strained smiles at all but instead are perfect conditions to show off the transformative, restorative grace of God, on Sunday mornings and every day that follows.

We don't need to build another addition on the Tower of Babel. We don't need to keep bowing down to self-sufficiency and the relentless drive to impress. We need to borrow the cup of sugar. We need to let the cracks show. We need the grace that saves wanderers like us. We need to drop-kick the cult of hustle-and-smile and instead let the world see the Gospel that is continually reaching into our clumsy need and changing us, present tense.

The world is hungry for a picture like that. The world is hungry for real-time, real-life conversation by the mailbox. It's hungry for the God we know by name, the God who doesn't step around our weakness or our failures or turn up His nose at our need for Him and for each other. The world is hungry for the power of the God of the harassed and helpless. His power is made perfect in our weakness. We are the broken *and* the redeemed, and we are His grateful kids made for this holy work. Hallelujah and may it ever be.

PART V

HORIZON

I HAVE REALLY GOOD NEWS FOR US: THE GRACE OF God will outlast every single thing on your list today. Maybe the list consists of things you have to do. Maybe it's a list of people you'd like to know, or people you wish you didn't. Maybe it's a list of grievances or hopes or worries or wins. Maybe it's a list of books you want to read or thank-you notes you should write or baby names you'd like to one day bestow.

Maybe it's a list of hurts so deep, you've never had to write them down because you just know. You suppose you'll always just know.

I don't know what's on the list you tucked next to your heart this morning, but I do know you have a list that you carry. I'm carrying mine too.

I also know that not too far into the future, my list will get too heavy for me to take with me. It always does. I can't support the weight of all the things I hope for or long for or regret or mourn. All the things on all my lists—those things only fit wholly in the palm of the One. His are the hands that formed us, and they are sure and capable and good. In God's hands, our lists don't weigh more than a single petal of our favorite spring bloom. And oh, how delicious it feels to hand over those burdens, straighten our curved spines and weary shoulders, and walk free.

Grace maps out a horizon of freedom. Lay down that list and reach for the better thing. Reach for grace. It's already here, so you don't even have to strain your eyes to find it. Open those eyes wide and I'll bet you hear yourself catch your breath because it's that kind of beautiful. It's a show stopper, this grace. And it's entirely, stunningly, amazingly all for you.

ENCORE

MY MOM IS A MUSICIAN. IN REAL LIFE. A LOT OF FOLKS *say* they are musicians. You, however, have watched *American Idol* auditions, so you know most people are very confused.

My mom swings the other way. She's a musical ninja but rather silent about it all. When my siblings and I were growing up, she never told us she was a marvel. She did tell us we should make sure to wear clean underwear in case of a car accident,[*] but nary a word about her upper fifth percentile of violin prowess. I didn't know that the soundtrack of my childhood was noteworthy until I went to college as a music major myself and walked the halls of the conservatory, listening to the manic scales of the string majors wafting out of practice rooms and into the corridor.

---

[*] The logic is still fuzzy here.

I remember squinting through the tiny windows, glimpsing furrowed, sweaty, sun-starved brows as they tried to whip those four strings into submission.

Hm.

My mom wasn't sweaty. She didn't furrow. She got nice and tan in the summer AND she sounded like a dream when she pulled her bow across those strings.

My mom was extraordinary and I never even knew it.* She played with all the greats in her forty years in the symphony: Ella Fitzgerald, Itzhak Perlman, Yo-Yo Ma, Josh Bell, Idina Menzel, Midori, Pinchas, Anne-Sophie. My siblings and I went along to most of those concerts. Lindsay looked like a Gap Kids model. Ryan was in agony, distraught to be inside on a Sunday afternoon and wearing a shirt with buttons. He would slide everything but his head off the upholstered theater seat and onto the ground by the end of the first movement. I brought a book and can't remember a single detail of 487 concerts.

In short, my mother's children are all ninnies. We didn't know! We lived with a genius and all we wanted was for her to make us Sloppy Joes!

There was one thing that would snap us out of our self-absorption and furtive whispers to Dad to let us skip out and go to Dairy Queen. Okay, two things. First, we liked watching the percussionist. He played at least eighteen instruments and he was very serious about all of them. He would start the rev-up to a single ding of the triangle at least twelve measures beforehand.

---

* If only we knew the gifts of our parents before we aged out of their daily care! CHILDREN OF MINE: YOUR DAD AND I ARE REALLY GREAT. BE IMPRESSED WITH US BY NEXT TUESDAY.

And he played the tympani like a man unleashed. We liked the drum guy.

And we liked the encore.

The encore didn't always happen, but when it did, even Ryan stopped rolling spitballs on the floor and sat up to watch. The encore piece happened only at the end of the official program and following sustained applause. The artist would wait in the wings after the last programmed piece, and if we clapped without ceasing (which is harder than it looks for (a) children and (b) all the octogenarians who attend the symphony), the performer would return to center stage, smile at the audience, and wait for the rustling to settle as we found our seats again. Sometimes the soloist would announce the title, but often he or she would just take a slow, deep breath and start in, bow across strings, fingers to keys, mouth to brass or reed. No extra fanfare, just a single line of notes rising out of the hushed silence, a song all of their choosing. No score on a music stand, no need for any extra reminders because the piece would have been memorized after years of gathering it in like an old friend, the music just waiting for a chance to soar into the space between us.

I DIDN'T EXACTLY make it to the encore in my own time as a music major. A beloved mentor, herself a musician, encouraged me to pursue music as a career only if I could not imagine myself being happy doing anything else. I could easily imagine other work that would fulfill me, more stable work, work that wouldn't require me to filet myself publicly all of my life, work that wouldn't demand self-promotion and constant competition with my peers.

The obvious choice was to bail on music and become a novelist.*

Plus, I was starting to feel like I might not belong in the music major crowd. They tended to get whipped up fairly easily, particularly my fellow vocal performance majors. One afternoon, for example, I was in line at the campus café, chatting with a theology professor I admired. This guy was a dear man, kind, thoughtful, super smart, patient with the snark and irreverence I used in order to mask my private worry about not getting this God thing right. Another student of his, an upperclassman vocal performance major I'd seen haunting the practice rooms, interrupted our conversation and approached the prof. She waved. The prof responded in kind, asked her how she was and about her class load that semester.

The Vocalist shook her head. She pointed to her throat, *which was covered by an actual ascot.* She mouthed, "I'm taking a vocal nap."

I changed my major, forthwith.

Maybe I'm not being generous enough. Maybe the Vocalist had solid reasons for disengaging from real-time life in order to save her energy for a hoped-for encore. Maybe she knew something I don't about being careful and reserving oneself and making deposits for later withdrawals.

But I doubt it. I think she missed out. That professor taught at the college for only a year. He was brilliant and his kindness a gift. She should have taken a chance and jumped into the conversation while she still could.

---

* See Proverbs 26:11.

✩ ✩ ✩

ALL THESE YEARS after my mom's Sunday concerts, I still love an encore. It's often my favorite part of the concert. The artist has the bulk of her work behind her. Nerves are gone. She trusts the audience and the audience loves her so much, they demand one more piece, one more moment with her. What if we gave each other the benefit of the encore? Just nix the audition, the proving yourself part, the part that makes us all feel like we are one bad entrance away from certain doom or at least sitting by ourselves at the lunch table?

Jesus did this all the time. He was the master of skipping straight to the encore, and it got Him into all sorts of trouble. Jesus wasn't preoccupied with the mess in front of Him. It wasn't that He didn't see the mess; brokenness abounded just as much in first-century Palestine as it does in twenty-first-century where we live. People were just as nutty and bossy and disrespectful and angry and worn and tired and pushy and ignorant and mean and lost then as they are now. Jesus saw all of that. It's just that instead of getting paralyzed by the overwhelming girth of the mess, He kept His eyes instead on where the messes were headed. Jesus had His eye on the encore.

Peter must have felt like he'd really blown it, denying he ever knew Jesus to save his own skin. Jesus, though, offered Peter breakfast on the beach. He knew the weight of Peter's epic failure, but He gently lifted it off his shoulders with a hot meal and a reminder of love times three. Peter had messed up a really big moment, right in the middle of the second act, but the encore was on its way, and I can just picture the twinkle in Jesus' eye as He told Peter to buckle up for the next scene.

Zaccheus must have felt like the gum on everyone's shoe, the short guy with a tall job, and the ability to use that job to oppress his own people. Jesus, though, saw a dinner invite and full restoration to a joy so big, Zaccheus couldn't even contain it.

The woman at the well must have felt the crushing press of aloneness, choosing to draw water in the blistering heat of midday instead of the morning when other women would gather. She was living in a mammoth relational mess, some of it probably made for herself and lots of inherited messes too. Jesus saw her full story, declared her freedom, and told her not to return to the chains that were familiar but destroying her. Go, freedom girl. Walk in that kind of light. And leave the darkness behind, no matter how comfortable it has become. She obeyed and became a lionhearted missionary, relentless in pulling her people out of the muck and onto new, vibrant ground.

Jesus gives us the wide, deep benefit of the doubt. He sees where we are headed and what we are becoming, even as we fall on our faces on a road, blinded and fumbling, waiting for clarity and for a mercy we don't deserve. We can't sidestep the mess, whether we made it or someone else made it for us. We need help navigating the fractured parts, the mudslides, the quicksand that binds us to old ways, ugly ways, enslaving ways. We don't do ourselves a favor by pretending the mess isn't there or by deciding to walk those stretches alone.

But we also don't stay in the practice room forever.

We don't rehearse and plan and fret about the performance. We don't take a vocal nap and miss the chance to use our voices today, now. Will we crash and burn? Maybe. Likely. But just like when my kids were toddlers and they would take a few first, tentative steps and then fall like drunken sailors, our good Father sees the tumble, scoops us up, and assures us that we haven't blown it forever. He's here. We're here. Grace is far sturdier than we are.

Jesus has already offered thunderous applause and is ready for the encore. In fact, I don't think He's one to wait until we've performed our socks off and have the blessing of the audience to play one more piece. I think He's more like Beethoven, who got such a rise out of the audience when he was conducting one of his final symphonies, after finishing the second movement of the concerto, he noticed people losing their minds with joy and started that movement over from the beginning and played it all over again.

God isn't waiting for our best work in order to decide if we're worth the price of the ticket. He's not the sour-faced critic in the balcony, the guy in a tweed jacket who came in late, leaves early, and sees the entire evening as something that didn't live up to its storied potential.

No. He is not the tweedy guy. God is the one in the first row, holding a massive bouquet of roses and raining them onto you before the conductor hits her very first downbeat. Bravo! He shouts as the petals make a carpet at your feet. I'm wild about you already, don't you know that? Sing your song! I'm the one who put it in your heart to begin with! Just don't forget that I'm already sold.

Read this out loud, please: I am God's beloved kid. I will dunk my head in the wild, rushing rivers of His grace. I delight in Him. I do not perform for Him.

Just like that achingly tender moment in the Bible when Jesus is baptized and God says what He thinks about His son, we get to bask in that same grace, that same rooting in what is true, all the way down. Jesus hadn't healed anybody yet. He hadn't preached a great sermon yet. He hadn't raised Lazarus, unleashed folks from demonic possession, turned water into wine. Those were all doozies, to be sure, but they were yet to come. God let loose with the roses before Jesus had done those things, and I think His timing was beautiful. Before everyone else started clamoring for Him, God was there, speaking over His boy in Matthew 3:17, saying what He had said to Him since the beginning of time, but now letting us eavesdrop: "This is My Son, My beloved, in Whom I delight!" (AMPC).

I can imagine the way Jesus must have breathed in those words, the way He would have reveled in that moment of remembering again who He was, who loved Him, who was pleased with His willingness to walk the entire road, start to finish. I can imagine He wants us to revel in that same baptism, that same coming up out of the dark and forsaking it for something so much better, the Best News that changes everything. God says to us too, "This is my beloved. Child, you bring me joy."

We are beloved, and we get the honor of joining the woman at the well as fetterless missionaries. Bravo, sons and daughters of the One and Only! Step into the light of His grace. You're right on time for the music written just for you.

The encore isn't the best saved for last. In fact, it's just the beginning.

NEW SPECS

PERHAPS THERE ARE NO MORE COMEDIC WORDS IN the English language than "birth plan." I just chortled out loud even reading those words. Incidentally, teenagers do not approve of their parents chortling. They prefer a demure smile. Maybe a slow nod of the head to acknowledge the presence of humor, but let's not go overboard or draw attention to the middle-aged in the room. Really, forget the chortle and the nod. Silence is best.

So I guess "birth plan" is just stage one of "parenting plan." Both are hilarious! Oh, how I wanted to plan for the birth of my children. Not one of them obeyed. Ana came a week later than promised. I was the approximate size of a beluga, but with the temperament of a manta. Mitch came a week early and so fast, the doc said that if I planned to have more children, I should check into the hospital three weeks before my due date, just to make sure I didn't accidentally drop a baby in the produce section of the grocery store. And Thea came at her leisure, dillydallying while Marc took a nap and I pretended to watch the Olympics, when suddenly she arrived with a vengeance, so quickly and decisively, the doctor didn't even make it down the hall before Nurse Sherry caught the kid. Marc was awake by then but only because I was shouting.

No birth plans. No toddler plans, or grade school plans or teenage plans. Perhaps young adult plans work? Not banking on it.

When I packed my cute little bag for Ana's delivery (CHORTLE CHORTLE), I included a CD of favorite tunes. I'd burned the CD myself. Billy Joel, James Taylor, maybe some Enya here and there. Welcome to the world, baby! Be calm as JT and Enya are calm!

I never even opened the case. "Just the Way You Are" didn't quite merge with "Someone extract this thing from me or the ship's going down!"

Another fun item in that hospital bag was a pair of black overalls I packed to wear home. Finally! Normal people clothes! I was pregnant in the era of the early 2000s, which was a dark day for maternity wear. Options were exactly horrible. The black overalls with the cute striped shirt underneath represented a return to normalcy. A return to fashion and cuteness and non-beluga.

On the day I was released, while Marc was having a total panic attack that they were going to just let us strap that child in a seat and take her home, no competency test required, I slipped the overalls out of my bag. Sure, Ana was squawking and red and seemed to be saying things we could not understand regarding her level of happiness. This was disappointing as it did not follow what we had been reading in the Baby Readiness Books. But at least I would look cute as I went home and started this plus-one adventure.

I couldn't get the overalls past my thighs, never mind the torso that still looked a heck of a lot like it had before the squawker had vacated her Airbnb.

Even though I was a slow learner, I was starting to see a pattern: The old way of doing things wasn't going to work anymore. A new era was dawning, the view was shifting by the minute, and I would need to look at things very, very differently.

I would also need new pants.

✩ ✩ ✩

MAYBE THERE ARE folks out there who like massive change around every bend, but I don't know them. Sure, some folks seek adventure as if it's a form of oxygen. I know nomads and wanderers and free spirits, and I love them all (I just make sure one of us has access to Google Maps). Even most nomads, though, love the constancy of friendship and the glories of a good meal every few hours or so. The scenery might change, but we do like some constants. A bed at night, a warm hand to hold, a friend to call even if we are on opposite sides of the world.

We don't love feeling the earth shift beneath our feet. We prefer some solid ground, math that makes sense, familiar mile markers for our days.

The thing is, a real encounter with grace messes up every last thing. The more we let God lift the veil on old ways of thinking and moving, the more we see things as they truly are instead of through the layers we've wallpapered on top. That coworker who drives you and your entire team bananas? The lens of grace doesn't allow you to dismiss her and even helps you see the beauty under the bananas. That family member who you really, really want to cut from the Christmas card list? The lens of grace doesn't give you the freebie. In fact, grace makes you gasp when you start to see how you and Cousin Crazypants share more than a gene pool. You're both wary and insecure and in need of someone to stay even when you're prickly. That church leader or schoolteacher or coach who wielded their position with too much bravado and not enough care? The lens of grace forces you to take a deep breath and remember your own shortcomings, not just when you were their age but last week. Yesterday. This very morning.

God reminds us over and over, sometimes to our wincing chagrin, that He is doing a new thing. He is paving a new way when He transforms your heart to look more like His, and that new way won't fit with the deep ruts you've been traveling all these years. You're going to need a new map. You're going to need to chuck most of the stuff you've packed and you're going to need something that will fit.

New wine needs new wineskins. Seeing your world through the eyes of grace might make you have to blink a little, but stick with it. The new view far outshines the old.

☆ ☆ ☆

I ONCE READ about a woman with something called tetrachro-macy.* This woman can see all sorts of things we can't, and she's not even a Marvel character.** While most of us have eyes that can register about one million different colors, people with tetrachro-macy can see *one hundred million* colors. The woman sees people wearing clashing colors on the regular, even though no one else seems bothered. She made her contractor bonkers when it took them thirty-two tries to get the right beige paint. Too yellow. Too blue. Too orange. Too pink, she said. The contractor saw only, um, beige.

She can't unsee the variety any more than we can see the dif-ferences between Beige Number 13 and Beige Number 32.

Grace is like that. When I spend time in the mornings read-ing and listening and learning from the One who made up grace to begin with, the rest of my days take an entirely different pal-ette of color. I see my own heart differently, more clearly, with both more honesty and more compassion. I see my family dif-ferently, and I can love them better, right where they stand or sit or collapse on the hardwood kitchen floor, which is the preferred and curious resting place of teenagers. I see my leaders, my col-leagues, my easy people, my tough people differently because I'm using a new map. The starting point of the day has grace written all over it, so the destination doesn't actually seem as immovable. In fact, I often have to toss out some of the stuff I had planned to

---

* Robson, David. "The Women with Superhuman Vision" BBC, September 4, 2014. https://www.bbc.com/future/article/20140905-the-women-with-super-human-vision.

** Please don't make me watch any more Marvel movies. Ever. How about a Dame Judi Dench marathon? Anybody?

schlep along because, it turns out, that stuff will only weigh me down.

When Marc and I moved to Costa Rica for a season, we had only one guidebook, printed on paper. At that time in history, we not only did not have mobile telephones, we also had only one single, solitary actual guidebook dedicated to Costa Rica. I'm not sure how this is possible, as I know we were not the first people to wonder about Costa Rica. Costa Ricans, for example, had been wondering for a good long while. Maybe other books existed but hadn't made their way to the northern climes of Minnesota?

At any rate, we disembarked from the plane, feeling that singular sensation of needing to run a mile, gulp fresh air, and eat a bowl of fruit one gets after air travel, and we started making our way toward the door and the lively city beyond. Again, due to the pioneer era in which we were journeying, we each had two suitcases that needed to be carried. With our hands. Two tiny wheels adorned the bottoms of each bag, but they were merely decorative. We lifted our bags, made our way out of the wild airport, and struck out into San José.

Our helpful guidebook named our destination as a cheap, moderately clean, cheap, and cheap hotel in which to spend our first night. Sold. We started out on foot, asking people along the way if we were on the right track. Definitely, they'd say, nodding. Just keep going in this direction and turn right at the gigantic chestnut tree.

Got it. Okay. The chestnut tree.

Roughly eight hundred hours and burned-out bi's and tri's later, we realized that the chestnut tree, while familiar to all locals, had been chopped down sometime near the end of the previous century. The hotel stood near the stump.

If we're going to enjoy the Grace Road that stretches out before us, we need new maps. The old ones won't work. The old language won't work. The old luggage won't work. The old mile markers won't work. We fix our eyes anew when we walk with Jesus. He has better ideas, and some of them are going to seem completely foreign to us until the veils start to fall and the scales on our eyes start to feel not only heavy but cumbersome.

This viewing the world through a grace lens really messes with our idea of ownership. We humans are really into owning stuff. Most of our wars, in fact, have been waged over possession. Possession of land, borders, resources, power, glory, even people. We like owning. We like putting our stamps on things, monogramming our rightful claims, calling things ours. We start this charade in the sandbox and we continue until we're in other, less colorful boxes with satin trim.

And just in case you're feeling a little smug because you're a minimalist and you don't care about land and power and glory, trust me, you also have a crush on owning things. Even if you're reading this in a yurt and you make your own cashew cheese and you don't believe in actual dollar bills, property tax, or reality TV, you are still greedy. You like having control of your time, your space, your freedom to do and be and say what you want. You like deciding what your resources are and how to use them to benefit you and your yurt.

We like having what's ours.

But grace topples the idea of what's ours by showing us a different way altogether. Everything we have is an undeserved gift. Everything we have isn't ours to begin with.

When I was in high school, my brave parents decided we should get some culture, already, and take a trip to Europe. We bought gigantic duffle bags and filled them to brimming with all the things we might need for ten days across the Atlantic. Three of the five of us were really worried about what people would think of us, so we packed with abandon. It was impossible to know if and when we would, say, stumble upon a prince or something. Our packing reflected this level of thoughtfulness. My parents were more measured, but on the early morning of our flight, when we converged at the minivan to load up, even they grunted when they hefted their bags into the trunk.

We parked at the econo-lot at the airport, shuffled ourselves and our gear across the crosswalk, and checked in. We were sweating, our hopes for Parisian chic already dashed. When the airline rep announced that our flight had been postponed to the following day, we did not cry. We did not complain. We did not mourn. We went home and took out half of the junk in our bags. The next day, we loaded that plane with deodorized armpits and only what we truly needed.

A life lived with a lens of grace does the same thing. Seeing the world grace-first helps us pack lighter, smarter. We realize more quickly that we don't need half the stuff we're lugging around, and we realize that what's left is all gifts anyway. When we start to see that our money is a gift wrapped in grace, the weight of it lightens immediately. The making and the keeping of money doesn't pull down our shoulders, hearts, and bodies anymore. Instead, we see it as something just passing through, a visitor we get to host in our home but only for a bit because its true worth comes in help and sustenance and blessing for others.

When we think about our time through a grace filter, we see that it, too, is a joy-drenched gift. We can't make more or less of it, so the best way to use it is wherever we can be couriers of grace. When we wonder if we have enough energy to do or be or try, the answer through the lens of grace is an unequivocal yes.

Grace says yes because it's looking at an entirely different map with entirely different colors and entirely different destinations. Grace is going to the best places, so we are wise to leave behind every lesser thing that's weighing us down.

Look, God says to our hearts. I'm doing a new thing. *You* are one of those new things. Trust me, He says, and you'll see colors you didn't know existed. Your view is about to get deeper and wider and more beautiful than you could have imagined when we started out. New, green paths in dead and forsaken wilderness, new rivers in the thirsty desert, new flesh over dry bones— I'm doing a new thing, and if you stick with me for a minute, you'll start to wonder what you ever saw in the old.

LAST DANCE

MY GREAT-GRANDMOTHER NELLIE DIED WHEN MY grandpa was still a boy. We have letters written in Nellie's careful penmanship. She writes about the winter, her failing health, the farm, the cold. There is ice on the inside of the walls, she says. The cold is unrelenting, she says.

We don't have a precise diagnosis for what made her sick and kept her sick, but we assume it was something that started innocently in her otherwise healthy body. Probably a virus or some sort of respiratory infection. Probably a version of the gunk all of us get who live in cold climates, something that irritates and annoys, robs us of sleep and clear breathing and exchanges for those good things headaches and a racking cough and aching bones. These days, we take ibuprofen to ease the discomfort.

We slam DayQuil to get through a meeting at work. We huddle under blankets and watch Netflix, waiting for the worst to pass, for our bodies to rebound, for the sickness to surrender to our robust immune systems and warm drinks and climate-controlled homes. We get better within a week and act like nothing ever happened.

Nellie didn't have access to all those creature comforts. Ice froze in rivulets on the walls of my great-grandmother's house. She had five children who needed care, and she became too sick to move. She died in that home. The wind continued to howl. She was only thirty-seven years old.

My grandpa put himself to bed those first nights and lay with tears rolling hot down his temples, onto his pillow. He was seven years old. This was a familiar but colorless detail in my family history until I had my own children. When Ana was seven, she went through a phase of crying in the middle of the day because she missed home. Her school was a five-minute walk from our kitchen, but home suddenly, dangerously felt too far away. When Mitch was seven, he wore tortoiseshell glasses and muscle shirts to show off his "guns." When Thea was seven, she had a contagious giggle, loved purple, and had a wide gap in front where her baby teeth used to be.

Seven is awfully young to be in your cold bedroom, trying to fall asleep while you sob. Seven is awfully young to think of a world without your momma.

This next part of the story came out years later, haltingly, as if my grandpa still wasn't sure if he should say it out loud. As he lay crying on one of those first hollow nights without his mom, fresh grief seeping into every corner of the room, someone came to sit at the foot of his bed. It wasn't his dad, not his brothers or his sister. Someone else. Someone kind. Someone warm, a stark contrast to both the winter in that space and the fear that gripped his heart.

The Someone looked at my grandpa and said, equal parts tenderness and sure, "You don't need to be afraid. You're going to be all right."

Years later, when Grandpa brushed the dust off this story and finally spoke it aloud to his family, he shook his head, remembering that moment with clarity even seven decades later. "I'm not sure if it was an angel or maybe Jesus Himself." He shrugged. "I just know He was there and that I believed Him."

Sounds like the most beautiful definition of grace, right there. God was there, and I believe what He said to me. I've done nothing to warrant a house call. I don't have my act together, and I haven't gussied myself up for Him. There's ice on the walls, for the love of Pete. Besides, the gussying doesn't move the needle anyway. I know that now, and I'm so grateful to report back that this is true as true. My grandpa seemed to be saying the same thing when he finally told us this story. I'm not sure about a lot of things, he said, and I don't know how this beautiful moment came to rise out of the ashes, but I do know two things. I know God was there, right there, right where I needed Him. And I know I believe what He said.

There was all sorts of pain ahead for my grandpa. His dad wasn't equipped to raise five kids on his own. Single Dad Support Group wasn't a thing and wouldn't be in that neck of the woods for at least another sixty years. My grandpa and his siblings were farmed out to aunts and uncles, raised by family that loved him but never quite leveled the wall between who were theirs by birthright and who were theirs by need. Grandpa would fight for his country in the skies over Europe, thousands of miles away from the rolling, green fields of the Midwest he called home. He would serve as an Air Force gunner in a B-17 bomber and be shot during combat over France, earning him a Purple Heart and a ticket home. He would marry and would complete one year of college before using his GI funds to build a painting business, raise five children of his own, be an elder in his church and a devoted fan of the Minnesota Twins. He would know pain and heartache and loss of many kinds. And through it all, he held this story, untouchable, within his heart and head.

Maybe he didn't say anything about his visitor for years because we are stoic Dutch people and we don't want our neighbors to think we think too much of ourselves. Who are we to claim a visit from the Most High? Maybe he feared that folks would think he'd gone Pentecostal or something, all that talk about intimate chitchat with the God of the universe.

Or maybe my grandpa knew what I know now too, that sometimes the One Who Sees makes it His mission to remind us He's near. Sometimes the God who died for us visits us and dispels the cold and the dark and replaces those smaller things with the overwhelming enough-ness of His very presence. Sometimes the King of all Kings comes near and low and holds us, even as He reminds us that only in Him can we forget about fear.

Don't be afraid, He says. You're going to be all right.

Look at me, kiddo.

We look.

And we believe what He says.

☆ ☆ ☆

MY FRIENDS KATHERINE and Jay are building the most extraordinary thing in the backwoods of Alabama. I say "backwoods" with all affection and a deeply rooted conviction that I will never move there unless Jesus makes me. It's not that the place itself isn't lovely; it is. Beautiful timbered acres, stretches of green fields, picturesque sunrises and sunsets over gentle hills, and a curving blue-green lake that's stocked with fish. The issue is that summers there, the only time I've visited, are so hot and humid, I start to take on a butchered Southern drawl and can only ask everyone I see if they are well hydrated. I become a very uninteresting person when the humidity shoots higher than 96 percent.

Katherine, Jay, their two sons, and a team of people who love them with a breathtaking ferocity strike out every summer to this spot in the backwoods. They open doors and windows, sometimes with a force and tenacity that belie their sweet Southern exteriors, and they carve out a space and time where families with disabilities can come and drink from a deep well of encouragement and respite. Every member of these families gets to be utterly, wholly themselves and utterly, wholly celebrated and loved. Katherine and Jay know well the long road of suffering in bodies that don't cooperate, and they know the unflagging pace of caring for those bodies. A week in the backwoods provides a wide spot in the road. Even in the heat, even through the muggy afternoons, the undercurrent of those days together is what Katherine calls a joy rebellion. Yes, we are pressed down but we are not crushed. Yes, we are weary but we are not destroyed. Yes, this road keeps twisting and turning, asking what feels like too much of us. But it is not too much. We don't cover these miles in isolation. We are an army of rebels, and we will not give one extra inch to a life void of joy.

The last night of camp, we gather for what Jay's sister Alex warned me would be "the best hour of my year." All of Jay's sisters look like they should be models for J.Crew. They have aristocratic cheekbones and unfairly thick, raven hair. I heard Alex's prediction, and I smiled, disbelieving. It was the heat, I thought. Or her surefire genetic connection to Camelot. She must be prone to hyperbole.

Alex was right. If anything, she undersold.

That night was a wild, hour-long, frenzy of joy. A DJ spun song after song, and we danced like the fools we are. Folks in wheelchairs did spins that defied physics. A beautiful boy who writes poetry and has no feet used the floor as a prop for his wicked dance moves. We made two lines and spot-lit kids who passed through, all of them shaking their groove thing, all of us grinning so widely, the muscles in our cheeks started to tremble.

I watched the faces around me, blurred images of uncontained joy. The rebellion was on. We were drawing lines. The battle was not over, but we were fully confident we were the victors.

I felt tears fall down my cheeks. I laughed, my heart beating wildly, matching the vibrating floor, the beat of the music.

My sweet buddy Sawyer grinned at me as he clutched my hands. I cried and laughed. He seemed perfectly at home with that mix of emotions. He knew firsthand about the strange bedfellows of pain and joy, of the waiting and the right-now.

Sawyer and I danced. The best hour of my week went too quickly.

Don't be afraid, I heard above the beautiful ruckus. Fear has no power here.

The voice got louder. I didn't have to strain to listen.

No more wasting time wondering about every step of the dance. Lay that burden down.

Look at me, kiddo.

Believe what I say.

MY GREAT-GRANDPA JOHN on the other side of the family pastored a small church in the northwest corner of Iowa. He preached two sermons each Sunday morning: one in English and one in Dutch. This bilingualism, sadly, died out by the time I was born into the fold. I do know a few Dutch words, but none of them can be said in church.

Great-grandpa John pastored for decades in that little church. He baptized, he counseled, he visited, he buried. He wrestled with Biblical texts and presented his findings to his congregation, sermon by sermon, every Sunday morning through frost and sunshine, turning leaves, and fledgling buds hard-won each spring.

John went Home at the age of ninety-five.* When asked what, if he could rewrite some of his story, he might have done differently in his lifetime of ministry, he said he wished he would have given more altar calls.

A lifetime of sermons, lived and spoken. Decades of study and teaching, sharing what he knew in two languages. And what

---

* My family tree is riddled with folks who made it to their late nineties. My sweet great-aunt Goldie died at 106. EVERY ONE OF THEM ATE HOMEMADE PIE, COOKIES, AND BARS UNTIL THE END. I feel we need to revisit the food pyramid.

did he wish he would have done more of? He wished he would have given more invitations to come forward at the end of a service, kneel together at the foot of the cross, and invite Jesus to rescue and redeem hearts in desperate need of Him.

I'm listening to my great-grandpa today and I'm saying this out loud to you, sweet, beautiful reader:

Jesus sees you. He sees the injury, the wrongs, both the ones you've inflicted and the ones you're carrying around that came at the hands of someone else.

Jesus knows you. He knows you have tried your best to shake off the weight of what you've done wrong and the weight of what you've done well. He knows your heart and all its broken spots. The weariness, the bitterness, the torn bits, the parts that don't even dare hope anymore.

Jesus is the one, the only one, to pluck your feet out of the mud, wash you in His reservoirs of mercy, and give you solid ground in exchange for the muck. He wants to walk with you to quiet waters, where He can restore your battered soul and pave the paths before and behind you with goodness and compassion.

Your part is small, just enough to hold in one hand. It's doable, easy enough for both a child and an ancient. Your part is to say yes. Yes, Jesus, I need You. Yes, I want You. Yes, You are enough. Yes, I am the zenith of Your creation and only You know how to bring out that beauty in me.

Yes.

You're here.

I don't need to be afraid anymore.

Grace falls down and lifts up, all in the same deep breath.

Yes. I'm with You in this joyful rebellion.

I'm laying down the extra. You carry it for me, please, because my spirit was never made for that kind of work.

Yes. I hear You above the noise.

I believe what You say.

Your grace that's brought me safe thus far is the same unflinching,

tireless,

tender and horizonless grace

that will lead me Home.

ACKNOWLEDGMENTS

I STARTED TRYING to wrap my head and heart around the idea of grace over twenty years ago. I don't have any cracked codes after all that time, but I certainly have been the recipient of grace in the wild over and over again, most notably during the writing of these pages.

I first spoke aloud my fledgling hope to write this book to my remarkable agent and friend, Andrea Heinecke. She has offered her unflagging confidence in me and my writing for years, and I count it an honor to work with her. I'm also grateful that she put the smackdown when I called her halfway through and whined, "What on earth am I doing, writing about grace? Who do I think I am? I'm bailing and will now take up crochet!" Andrea rightly told me to back away from the crochet hooks, get a grip, and keep writing. Crochet hooks have sharp points, after all, and a life of grace typically precludes a life of violence.

Beth Adams, Daisy Hutton, Emma Smith, Luria Rittenberg, Kristen Andrews, Whitney Hicks, Gabriella Wikidal, Patsy Jones, Katie Robison, Cat Hoort, Kaitlin Mays, Ellie Long, and the rest of the extraordinary team at Worthy/Hachette have championed this book start to finish, even when I wigged out about having my eighth-grade graduation photo on the cover. Thank you for your hard work on my behalf and for ignoring my pleas to swap my photo for one of Jennifer Garner.

Nicole Baart and Tosca Lee have given their whole hearts to me in friendship, cheerleading, commiseration, and crashes at the Lincoln Sanctum. Thank you, intrepid girls, for walking these many years shoulder to shoulder.

The Oaks team makes everything better. Everything. Which is why my plan is to move there permanently and pitch a modest tent at the top of the yellow slide. I'll take over coffee duty! Holly Anderson, Megan Tibbits, Rossie Robertson, Jessica Who Makes Sublime Granola, and the many interns who have made that spot a second home for me all deserve applause and a kick line.

Taylor Hughes has absorbed wailing and gnashing of writerly teeth. That he does this while also making a fainting goat disappear only underscores his brilliance as an illusionist and his deep reservoirs of friendship.

The Oaks has also given me circles upon circles of fellow writing compatriots. I am ever grateful to them and to our coaching family for the chance to hear your stories, enter in and celebrate together at words well won.

Jody Luke and Drew Fountain include me in work that matters deeply. Thank you both for saving me a seat. Stephanie Wesson is a marvel who keeps plates spinning in ways that defy gravity. She is also a dear friend. I am indebted to her, Patrick Dodd, Jordan Cragg, Marissa Alford, and to the entire crew of remarkable people who make our work a place of welcome and wonder.

Betsy De Glopper, Anne Summers, and Suzy Lowe infuse our efforts with joy and purpose. Thank you, you three, for helping me remember why we do what we do. Thank you, too, for forgiving me for every email that begins "I'm sorry for my delay." I owe you donuts (GF for Bets).

Stefanie, Justin, and Ellie Boyce are real-life, heart-expanding evidence of the grace of God in my life. I adore you three so much, it hurts. See you on the dock.

Adam and Kaitlyn, Lindsey and Jon, Richard and Ashley, thank you for your friendship, your steadfast kindness, and for continuing to invite me into your adventuring.

Maria Goff, you grow beautiful spaces, a beautiful family, and a beautiful life. Thank you for praying for me, laughing with me, and for putting out the welcome mat over and over to your friendship. And for the olive-green Oaks jacket. I know I have arrived because I have that jacket. Bury me in it.

Bob Goff, you are the best fire starter and also the best fire tender. You assume I can do extraordinary things, and then you clear the path, even when I'm yipping, "Wait, what? Shouldn't we talk about this?" You make me laugh until I wheeze, which is one of my most unflagging love languages, and our work together has been profound joy and the best surprise. May you feel to your bones the gratitude I and so many others have for you, as well as the delight and love of the One you adore.

To the Sarahs (Hanson and Denhart): Thank you for hundreds of hours, words, and prayers absorbed and set free on my behalf. I know the treasure I have in you.

Thank you to Makila Lors for years of friendship and for checking in with kindness, loyalty, and hand-painted notes that tell me she loves me. Love you too.

Ryan, Betsy, Olivia, and Jonah Beach have weathered decades with our crew, sunny skies and moonlit boat rides as well as strong winds and rocky shores. Their boundless generosity of spirit, time, and love sustains us and holds us fast.

Thank you to my siblings, who seem to still like me even after all those years of me being a punk. Ry and Linds, you are two of the reasons I know God loves me more than I deserve. Thank you, too, to my gigantic and extended family. You have loved me through all seasons, and my happiest days are when we are all together and armed with rhubarb pie and almond patties.

Mom and Dad, your lives are a master class on grace. Thank you for being people who are quick to listen, quick to apologize, quick to pray, and quick to laugh. That medley might just be the secret sauce of lives well lived.

Ana, Mitch, and Thea, you three are really fantastic people. I'm not sure how you pulled this off, considering your maternal influence, but I'm very grateful you are who you are. I love you three and shake my head at the bounty I have in you.

Marc, just when I think you can't surprise me anymore with the way you love me, you smatter that idea to bits. My heart still races when you grin at me, and I will never get over the embarrassment of German-Norwegian riches I have in you. Love you fiercely and always.

God of infinite, head-shaking, unstoppable, bottomless grace, I am Yours, we are Yours, because You say so. Thank you for saying so.

ABOUT THE AUTHOR

Kimberly Stuart is a writer, speaker, and podcaster. She is the author of eight novels and has made her home in Minneapolis, Houston, Chicago, Costa Rica, Nebraska, and Iowa, where she now lives with her brave husband and three wily children.